The ESSENTIALS® of

European History

1789 – 1848
Revolution & the
New European Order

John W. Barrett, Ph.D.

Chair and Professor of Social Sciences
Marywood College
Scranton, Pennsylvania

D0190638

Research & Education Association
61 Ethel Road West
Piscataway, New Jersey 08854

THE ESSENTIALS®
OF EUROPEAN HISTORY
1789 to 1848
Revolution and the New European Order

Printed in the United States of America

Library of Congress Catalog Card Number 98-68780

International Standard Book Number 0-87891-708-X

What the "Essentials of History" Will Do for You

REA's "Essentials of History" series offers a new approach to the study of history that is different from what has been available previously. Each book in the series has been designed to steer a sensible middle course, by including neither too much nor too little information.

Compared with conventional history outlines, the "Essentials of History" offer far more detail, with fuller explanations and interpretations of historical events and developments. Compared with voluminous historical tomes and textbooks, the "Essentials of History" offer a far more concise, less ponderous overview of each of the periods they cover.

The "Essentials of History" are intended primarily to aid students in studying history, doing homework, writing papers and preparing for exams. The books are organized to provide quick access to information and explanations of the important events, dates, and persons of the period. The books can be used in conjunction with any text. They will save hours of study and preparation time while providing a firm grasp and insightful understanding of the subject matter.

Instructors too will find the "Essentials of History" useful. The books can assist in reviewing or modifying course outlines. They also can assist with preparation of exams, as well as serve as an efficient memory refresher.

In sum, the "Essentials of History" will prove to be handy reference sources at all times.

The authors of the series are respected experts in their fields. They present clear, well-reasoned explanations and interpretations of the complex political, social, cultural, economic and philosophical issues and developments which characterize each era.

In preparing these books REA has made every effort to assure their accuracy and maximum usefulness. We are confident that each book will prove enjoyable and valuable to its user.

Dr. Max Fogiel, Program Director

About the Author

John W. Barrett is currently professor and chairperson of the undergraduate department of social science at Marywood College in Scranton, Pennsylvania, where he has held numerous teaching posts since 1960. He holds a bachelor's degree in history and English, a master's degree in history and political science, and a Ph.D. from Georgetown University in history and international diplomacy. Further graduate study in history and interdisciplinary social sciences was completed at various colleges and universities. Additionally, his public school administrative certification was received from Lehigh University.

Dr. Barrett maintains memberships in numerous professional organizations and national honor fraternities. He has been listed in *Directory of American Scholars*, *Community Leaders of America*, and *Outstanding Leaders of America*.

CONTENTS

Chapter No.		Page No.
1	THE FRENCH REVOLUTION I, 1789 – 1799	1
1.1	Impact of the Scientific Revolution (c. 1500 – 1700)	2
1.1.1	Pioneers	2
1.1.2	Philosophical Trends	3
1.1.3	Consequences	3
1.2	Influence of the Enlightenment (c. 1700 – 1800)	4
1.2.1	The Philosophes: Agents of Change	4
1.2.2	Major Assumptions of the Enlightenment	5
1.2.3	Enlightenment Effect on Society	6
1.2.4	Era of "Enlightened Despotism"	7
1.3	Influence of the American Revolution	8
1.4	Causes of the French Revolution	9
1.4.1	Cumulative Discontent with the Ancient Regime	9
1.4.2	Immediate Cause: Financial Mismanagement	10
1.4.3	Estates General Summoned	11
1.5	Phases of Revolution	12
1.5.1	The National Assembly, 1789 – 1791	12
1.5.2	The Legislative Assembly, 1791 – 1792	14
1.5.3	The National Convention, 1792 – 1795	15
1.5.4	The Directory, 1795 – 1799	17
1.6	Evaluation	18
1.6.1	European Reaction to the Events of 1789 – 1799	18
1.6.2	Results	18
2	THE FRENCH REVOLUTION II, THE ERA OF NAPOLEON, 1799 – 1815	19
2.1	Background of Napoleon's Life	19
2.2	Role in Directory Government, 1795 – 1799	20

2.3	Consulate Period, 1799 – 1804	
	(Enlightened Reform)	21
2.3.1	Domestic Accomplishments	21
2.4	Empire Period, 1804 – 1814 (War and Defeat)	22
2.4.1	Restoration of Monarchy	22
2.4.2	Militarism and Empire Building	22
2.5	Evaluation	24

3	**THE POST-WAR SETTLEMENT: THE CONGRESS OF VIENNA, 1814 – 1815**	**26**
3.1	Personalities	26
3.1.1	The "Big Four"	26
3.1.2	The "Dancing Congress"	27
3.2	Principles of Settlement: Legitimacy, Compensation, Balance of Power	28
3.3	Enforcement Provisions (Concert of Europe)	29
3.3.1	Congress System	30
3.4	Evaluation	30

4	**THE INDUSTRIAL REVOLUTION**	**32**
4.1	England Begins the Revolution in Energy and Industry	33
4.1.1	Early Progress	34
4.2	Spread of Industrialization to Europe and the World	35
4.2.1	The Challenges to the Spread of Industrialism	36
4.2.2	Route of Industrialization	36
4.3	Growth of Industrial Society	36
4.3.1	The Bourgeoisie: The New Aristocracy	37
4.3.2	The Factory Worker: The New Wage-Earning Class	37
4.4	Social Effects of Industrialization	38
4.5	Evaluation	39

5	**IMPACT OF THOUGHT SYSTEMS (ISMS) ON THE EUROPEAN WORLD**	**40**
5.1	Romanticism	40
5.1.1	Characteristics	41
5.1.2	Romantic Literature, Art, Music, and Philosophy	41
5.1.3	Impact	43
5.2	Conservatism	43
5.2.1	Characteristics	43
5.2.2	Impact	44
5.3	Liberalism	44
5.3.1	Characteristics	45
5.3.2	Early Nineteenth Century Advocates of Liberalism	47
5.3.3	Impact	47
5.4	Nationalism	47
5.4.1	Characteristics	48
5.4.2	Impact of Nationalism	48
5.4.3	Evaluation	49
5.5	Socialism	50
5.5.1	Characteristics	50
5.6	Evaluation	53
6	**EUROPE IN CRISIS, 1815 – 1833: REPRESSION, REFORM AND REVOLUTION**	**54**
6.1	Post-War Repression, 1815 – 1820	55
6.1.1	England	55
6.1.2	France	56
6.1.3	Austria and the German States	57
6.1.4	Russia	59
6.2	Revolutions I, 1820 – 1829	60
6.2.1	The International System: The Concert of Europe	60
6.2.2	The Revolutions of the 1820s	62
6.2.3	England Chooses Reform Over Revolution	64
6.3	Revolutions II, 1830 – 1833	65
6.3.1	France: The July Revolution	66

6.3.2	The Belgian Independence Movement (1830 – 1831)	67
6.3.3	Poland (1830 – 1831)	67
6.3.4	Italy (1831 – 1832)	68
6.3.5	Germany (1830 – 1833)	68
6.3.6	Great Britain: Reform Continues	68
6.4	Evaluation	69
7	**THE REVOLUTIONS OF 1848**	**70**
7.1	Causes	70
7.2	Republicanism: Victory in France and Defeat in Italy	72
7.2.1	France: The Second Republic and Louis Napoleon	72
7.2.2	Italy: Republicanism Defeated	73
7.3	Nationalism Resisted in Austrian Empire	74
7.3.1	Vienna	75
7.3.2	Bohemia	76
7.3.3	Hungary	76
7.3.4	Italy	77
7.4	Liberalism Halted in the Germanies	78
7.4.1	Prussia, The Frankfurt Parliament and German Unification	78
7.5	Great Britain and the Victorian Compromise	80
7.5.1	Highlights of the "Compromise Era"	80
7.6	Evaluation	82
8	**EPILOGUE: THE VIEW FROM MID-NINETEENTH CENTURY EUROPE**	**84**

CHAPTER 1

THE FRENCH REVOLUTION I, 1789 – 1799

The shape of the modern world first became visible during ten years of upheaval in France between the years 1789 and 1799. Radical ideas about society and government were developed during the 18th century in response to the success of the "scientific" and "intellectual" revolutions of the preceding two centuries. Armed with new scientific knowledge of the physical universe as well as a new view of the human capacity to detect "truth," social critics assailed the existing modes of thought governing political, social, religious and economic life.

Thus the modern world that came of age in the 18th century was characterized by rapid, revolutionary changes which paved the way for economic modernization and political centralization throughout Europe. The ideas and institutions created by the revolutionaries would be perpetuated and extended by Napoleon Bonaparte, who conquered and converted Europe.

1.1 IMPACT OF THE SCIENTIFIC REVOLUTION (c. 1500 – 1700)

The Scientific Revolution revolutionized human thinking about the physical universe and themselves by producing a body of independent, scientific knowledge based on new measuring devices and new methods of observation and interpretation. This knowledge suggested that humans would understand the operation of the physical world through use of their reason, aided by the modern scientific method of inquiry.

The "scientific method" involved identifying a problem or question, forming a hypothesis (unproven theory), making observations, conducting experiments, interpreting results with mathematics and drawing conclusions.

1.1.1 *Pioneers*

Nicolaus Copernicus (1473 – 1543) rejected the geocentric (earth-centered) view of universe and suggested a heliocentric (sun-centered) view of the universe and thus began the tradition of modern scientific thinking.

Galileo Galilei (1564 – 1642) developed a powerful telescope and confirmed Copernicus' theories.

Tycho Brahe (1546 – 1601) is considered the greatest astronomer of the late 16th century. Having built one of the earliest modern observatories, he kept meticulous celestial observations.

Johannes Kepler (1571 – 1630) used Brahe's observations to prove that a mathematical order existed in the planetary system; he proved mathematically that the planets revolve around the sun.

Isaac Newton (1642 – 1727) discovered the laws of motion, gravity and inertia. By building on earlier discoveries he developed a systematic interpretation of the operation of the universe (Newtonian View of the Universe), wherein natural scientific laws all worked together to provide a clear and comprehensive explanation of the physical universe. After Newton, the scientific method was not a matter of theory or observation, but both. Little wonder then that the poet Alexander Pope could write: "Nature and nature's laws lay hid in the night; God said, Let Newton be! and all was light."

1.1.2 *Philosophical Trends*

Empiricism (inductive method of reasoning) was advanced by Sir Francis Bacon (1561 – 1626), who believed knowledge was gained through systematic observation of the world and tested by experiment.

Rationalism (deductive method of reasoning) was advanced by René Descartes (1596 – 1650), who rejected the senses as a basis for knowledge and argued that reality could be known only by reasoning from self-evident axiomatic principles: *"Cogito ergo sum"* ("I think, therefore I am").

1.1.3 *Consequences*

The Scientific Revolution gave birth to the modern scientific community, whose goal was the expansion of knowledge based on modern scientific method that rejected traditional knowledge.

It likewise convinced many persons that all the complexities of the universe (including human relations) could be reduced to relatively simple mechanical laws such as those found in the physical universe.

1.2 INFLUENCE OF THE ENLIGHTENMENT (c. 1700 – 1800)

The Scientific Revolution gravely undermined the foundation on which the traditional social order of the 18th century rested by producing a revolution in the world of ideas which would seriously challenge the status quo. The enlightenment was a response to economic and political changes at work in European society and heralded the coming of a new secular society.

1.2.1 *The Philosophes: Agents of Change*

The new learning was promoted by a relatively small number of thinkers called philosophes — not philosophers in a traditional sense but social activists for whom knowledge was something to be converted into reform. They were not always original thinkers but popularizers of leading reformist thought. The philosophes believed their task was to do for human society what the scientists had done for the physical universe: apply reason to society for the purpose of human improvement and in the process discover the natural laws governing God, humans and society.

While they came from virtually every country in Europe, most of the famous social activists were French, probably because France was the center of this intellectual revolution.

Voltaire (1694 – 1778), considered the most brilliant and influential of the philosophes, argued for tolerance, reason, limited government and free speech.

Denis Diderot (1713 – 1784) served as editor of the *Encyclopedia*, the bible of the enlightenment period. This twenty-eight volume work was a compendium of all new learning; no self-respecting reformer would be found without a set.

Baron de Montesquieu (1689 – 1756) authored *The Spirit of the Laws* (1748) in which the separation of powers theory was found. Montesquieu believed such a separation would keep any individual (including the king) or group (including the nobles) from gaining total control of the government.

Jean Jacques Rousseau (1712 – 1778) wrote *The Social Contract* (1762) in an attempt to discover the origin of society and propose the composition of the ideal society which, he believed, was based on a new kind of social contract.

The dissemination of enlightenment thought was largely accomplished through philosophes touring Europe or writing and printing books and essays, the publication of the *Encyclopedia* (1751), and the discussions in the salons of the upper classes. The salons became the social setting for the exchange of ideas, and were usually presided over by prominent women.

1.2.2 *Major Assumptions of the Enlightenment*

Human progress was possible by changing the environment, i.e., better people, better societies, better standard of living.

Humans were free to use reason to reform the evils of society.

Material improvement would lead to moral improvement.

Natural science and human reason will discover the meaning of life.

Laws governing human society would be discovered through application of the scientific method of inquiry.

Inhuman practices and institutions would be removed from society in a spirit of humanitarianism.

Human liberty would ensue as individuals became free to choose what reason dictated or required as good.

1.2.3 Enlightenment Effect on Society

Changes or reform must be instituted when institutions cannot demonstrate a rational base of operation.

Religion. Deism or "natural religion" was inaugurated, which rejected traditional Christianity by promoting an impersonal God who does not interfere in the daily lives of the people. The continued discussion of the role of God led to a general skepticism associated with Pierre Bayle (1647 – 1706), a type of religious skepticism pronounced by David Hume (1711 – 1776), and a theory of atheism or materialism advocated by Baron Holbach (1723 – 1789).

Political Theory. John Locke (1632 – 1704) and Jean Jacques Rousseau (1712 – 1778) believed that people were capable of governing themselves either through a political (Locke) or social (Rousseau) contract forming the basis of society. However, most philosophes opposed democracy, preferring a limited monarchy sharing power with the nobility.

Economic Theory. The assault on mercantilist economic theory was begun by the physiocrats in France, who proposed a "laissez-faire" (non-governmental interference) attitude toward land usage, and culminated in the theory of economic capitalism associated with Adam Smith (1723 – 1790) and his slogans of free trade, free enterprise and the law of supply and demand.

Educational Theory. Attempting to break away from the strict control of education by the church and state, Jean Jacques Rousseau advanced the idea of progressive education where children learn by doing and where self-expression is encouraged. This idea was carried forward by Johann Pestalozzi, Johann

Basedow and Friedrich Frobel and influenced a new view of childhood.

Psychological Theory. In the *Essay Concerning Human Understanding* (1690) John Locke offered the theory that all human knowledge was the result of sensory experience without any preconceived notions, because the mind at birth was a blank slate (tabula rasa) that registered the experience of the senses passively. Education was critical in determining human development. Human progress is in the hands of society.

Gender Theory. The assertion of feminist rights evolved through the emergence of determined women who had been denied access to formal education, yet used their position in society to advance the cause of female emancipation. The enlightenment salons of Madame de Geoffren and Louise de Warens are an example of self-educated women taking their place alongside their male counterparts. One woman fortunate enough to receive education in science was Emilie du Chatelet, an aristocrat trained as a mathematician and physicist. Her scholarship resulted in the translation of Newton's work from Latin into French. The writing of Lady Mary Montagu and Mary Wollstonecraft promoted equal political and educational rights for women. Madame Marie Roland was a heroic figure throughout the early but critical periods of the French Revolution as she attacked the evils of the Ancien Regime.

1.2.4   Era of "Enlightened Despotism"

Most philosophes believed human progress and liberty would ensue as absolute rulers became "enlightened." The rulers would still be absolute but use their power benevolently as reason dictated. Their reforms were usually directed at increasing their power rather than the welfare of their subjects. Their creed was "Everything for the people, nothing by the people."

Most of the philosophes opposed democracy. According to Voltaire, the best form of government was a monarchy in which the rulers shared the ideas of the philosophes and respected the people's rights. Such an "enlightened" monarch would rule justly and introduce reforms. Voltaire's influence, as well as that of other philosophes, on Europe's monarchs produced the "enlightened despots" who nonetheless failed to bring about lasting political change. Some famous "despots" included Frederick "the Great" of Russia (1740 – 1786), Catherine "the Great" of Russia (1762 – 1796), and Joseph II of Austria (1765 – 1790).

1.3   INFLUENCE OF THE AMERICAN REVOLUTION

The American Revolution acted as a "shining beacon" to Europeans anxious for change, and helped prove that people could govern themselves without the help of monarchs and privileged classes.

France, the center of Enlightenment thought, was particularly vulnerable. Eighteenth-century ideas about the "Rights of Man" and the "Consent of the Governed" were discussed widely in French salons as well as in the rest of Europe. French reformers believed their nation was a perfect example of everything wrong with society. Philosophes and their admirers were galvanized into action.

Finally, the concept of revolution was validated as a legitimate means to procure social and political change when it could not be effected through existing avenues. However, the American Revolution was not a radical revolution but rather a conservative movement: It preserved the existing social order and property rights, and led to a carefully thought-out constitutional system built on stability and continuity.

1.4 CAUSES OF THE FRENCH REVOLUTION

1.4.1 *Cumulative Discontent with the Ancient Regime*

The rising expectations of "enlightened" society were demonstrated in the increased criticism directed toward government inefficiency and corruption or toward the privileged classes. The social stratification model failed to correspond to the realities of wealth and ability in French society: The clergy (First Estate) and nobility (Second Estate), representing only two percent of the total population of twenty-four million, were the privileged classes and were essentially tax exempt. The remainder of the population (Third Estate) consisted of the middle class, urban workers and the mass of peasants, and all bore the entire burden of taxation and the imposition of feudal obligations. As economic conditions worsened in the 18th century, the French state became poorer and totally dependent on the poorest and most depressed sections of the economy for support at the very time this tax base had become saturated.

The mode of absolute government practiced by the Bourbon dynasty was wed to the "Divine Right of Kings" philosophy. This in turn produced a government that was irresponsible and inefficient, with a tax system that was unjust and inequitable, and without any means of redress because of the absence of any meaningful representative assembly. The legal system was chaotic, with no uniform or codified laws.

The economic environment of the 18th century produced a major challenge to the state-controlled French economy (mercantilism), as businessmen and bankers assailed the restrictive features of this economic philosophy. With the growth of new industrial centers and the philosophic development of modern capitalist thought, the middle classes began to assert themselves, demanding that their economic power be made commensurate with political and social power – both of which were denied them. Within France, the estate system allowed the few to monopolize all economic benefits, while the many were "invisible." Thus, an inequitable and inefficient tax system haunted those least able to pay, while the mass of peasants had an additional burden – that of performing feudal obligations for the privileged classes as well as the payment of outdated feudal taxes and fees.

The intellectual currents of the 18th century were responsible for creating a climate of opposition based on the political theories of John Locke, Jean Rousseau, Baron Montesquieu and other philosophes; the economic ideas of the French physiocrats and Adam Smith (the "Father of Modern Capitalism"); and the general reform-minded direction of the century.

1.4.2 Immediate Cause: Financial Mismanagement

The coming of revolution seemed a paradox in a nation that was one of the largest and richest nations in the world, with a population around twenty-four million and a capital city (Paris) which was considered the crossroads of Enlightenment civilization. Dissatisfaction with the way France was administered reached a critical stage during the reign of King Louis XVI (1774 – 1792).

The deepening public debt was of grave concern, and resulted from (1) the colonial wars with England, 1778 – 1783; (2) French participation in the American War of Independence; (3) maintaining large military and naval establishments; and (4) the extravagant costs of maintaining the Royal Court at Versailles. Unable to secure loans from leading banking houses in Europe (due to poor credit rating), France edged closer to bankruptcy.

Between 1730 and the 1780s, there was an inflationary spiral which increased prices dramatically while wages failed to adjust accordingly. Government expenses continued to outstrip tax revenues. The "solution" to the debt problem was to either increase the rates of taxation or decree new taxes. The French tax system could not produce the amount of taxes needed to save the government from bankruptcy because of the corruption and inefficiency of the system. The legal system of "Parlements" (Courts), controlled by the nobility, blocked tax increases as well as new taxes in order to force the king to share power with the Second Estate.

As France slid into bankruptcy, Louis XVI summoned an Assembly of Notables (1787) in the mistaken hope they would either approve the king's new tax program or consent to the removal of their exemption from the payment of taxes. They refused to agree to either proposal.

1.4.3 Estates General Summoned

Designed to represent the three estates of France, this ancient feudal body had only met twice, once at its creation in 1302 and again in 1614. When the French parlements insisted that any new taxes must be approved by this body, King Louis XVI reluctantly ordered it to assemble at Versailles by May, 1789. Each estate was expected to elect their own representatives. As a gesture to the size of the Third Estate, the king doubled the number of their representatives. However, the Parlement of Paris decreed that voting in the Estates General would follow "custom and tradition," i.e., by estate unit voting. Therefore the First and Second estates, with similar interests to protect, would control the historic meeting despite the increased size of the Third Estate.

Election fever swept over France for the very first time. The 1788 – 89 election campaign is sometimes considered the precursor of modern politics. Each estate was expected to compile a list of suggestions and complaints called "cahiers" and present them to the king. These lists of grievances emphasized the need for reform of government and civil equality. Campaigning focused on debate and the written word (pamphlets). The most influential writer was the Abbé Siéyès and his pamphlet, "What is the Third Estate?"; the answer was "everything."

The election campaign took place in the midst of the worst subsistence crisis in 18th century France, with widespread bad harvests, grain shortages and inflated bread prices.

Finally, on May 5, 1789 the Estates General met and was immediately convulsed over the voting method, i.e., voting by unit and not per capita. Each estate was ordered to meet and vote separately. The third estate refused and insisted on the entire assembly remaining together.

1.5 PHASES OF REVOLUTION

1.5.1 *The National Assembly, 1789 – 1791*

After a six-week deadlock over voting methods, the Third Estate declared itself the true National Assembly of France (June 17). They were immediately locked out of their meeting place by order of Louis XVI. Instead they assembled in an indoor tennis court where they swore an oath never to disband until they had given France a constitution (Tennis Court Oath). The third estate had assumed sovereign power on behalf of the nation. Defections from the First and Second Estates then caused the king to recognize the National Assembly (June 27) after dissolving the Estates General. At the same time, Louis XVI ordered troops to surround Versailles.

The "Parisian" revolution began at this point. Angry because of food shortages, unemployment, high prices, and fearing military repression, the workers and tradesmen began to arm themselves. On July 14 they stormed the ancient fortress of the Bastille in search of weapons. The fall of this hated symbol of royal power gave the revolution its baptism of blood. The king recalled his troops from Versailles. The spirit of rebellion spread to the French countryside, triggered by a wave of rumor and hysteria. A feeling of fear and desperation called "The Great Fear" took hold of the people. They attacked the symbols of the upper class wealth, the manor houses, in an effort to destroy the legal records of their feudal obligations. The middle class responded to this lower class violence by forming the National Guard Militia to protect property rights. Hoping to put an end to further violence, the National Assembly voted to abolish feudalism in France and declare the equality of all classes (August 4). A virtual social revolution had taken place peacefully. The assembly then issued a constitutional blueprint, the "Declaration of the Rights of Man and Citizens" (August 26), a guarantee of due process of law and the sovereignty of the people. The National Assembly now proceeded to its twin functions of governing France on a day-to-day basis and writing a constitution.

Among the achievements of the National Assembly were the following:

1) *Secularization of Religion* — Church property was confiscated to pay off the national debt. The Civil Constitution of the Clergy (1790) created a national church with 83 bishops and a like number of dioceses. All clergy were to be democratically elected by the people and have their salaries paid by the state. The practical result was to polarize the nation over the question of religion.

2) *Governmental Reform* — To make the country easier to administer, the Assembly divided the country into 83

departments (replacing the old provincial boundary lines) governed by elected officials. With a new system of law courts, France now had a uniform administrative structure, 83 dioceses, departments and judicial districts.

3) *Constitutional Changes* — Despite a failed attempt by Louis XVI and his family to escape from France (June 20, 1791) and thereby avoid approving the Constitution of 1791, the National Assembly completed what may have been its greatest task by transforming France into a constitutional monarchy with a unicameral Legislative Assembly. Middle class control of the government was assured through an indirect method of voting and property qualifications.

1.5.2 *The Legislative Assembly, 1791 – 1792*

While the National Assembly had been rather homogeneous in its composition, the new government began to reflect the emergence of political factions in the revolution who were competing for power. The most important political clubs were republican groups such as the Jacobins (radical urban) and Girondins (moderate rural), while the Sans-culottes (working-class extreme radical) were a separate faction with an economic agenda.

The focus of political activity during the ten-month life of the Legislative Assembly was the question of "war." Influenced by French nobles who had fled France beginning in 1789 (Émigrés), the two largest continental powers, Prussia and Austria, issued the Declaration of Pillnitz (August, 1791) declaring the restoration of French monarchy as their goal. With a sharply polarized nation, mounting political and economic chaos, and an unpopular monarch, republican sentiment gained strength as war against all monarchs was promoted to solve domestic problems. Ideological fervor and anti-Austrian sentiment drove the

Legislative Assembly to declare war on Austria (April, 1792). Unprepared, the French revolutionary forces proved no match for the Austrian military. The Jacobins blamed their defeat on Louis XVI, believing him to be part of a conspiracy with Prussia and Austria. Mobs reacted to the threat made by the invading armies to destroy Paris (Brunswick Manifesto) if any harm came to the royal family by seizing power in Paris and imprisoning the king. The Legislative Assembly came under attack and obliged the radicals by suspending the 1791 Constitution, ordering new elections based on universal male suffrage for the purpose of summoning a national convention to give France a republican form of government.

1.5.3 *The National Convention, 1792 – 1795*

Meeting for the first time in September, 1792, the Convention abolished monarchy and installed republicanism. Louis XVI was charged with treason, found guilty and executed on January 21, 1793. Later the same year, the queen, Marie Antoinette would meet the same fate.

By the spring of 1793 the new republic was in a state of crisis. England and Spain had joined Austria and Prussia in opposing the revolution. Food shortages and counterrevolution in western France threatened the radicals' grip on the revolution. A power struggle ensued between Girondins and Jacobins until the Jacobins ousted their political enemy and installed an emergency government to deal with the external and internal challenges to the revolution. A Committee of Public Safety, directed by Maximilien Robespierre, responded to the food shortages and related economic problems by decreeing a planned economy (Law of the Maximum) which would also enable France to urge total war against its external enemies. Lazare Carnot, known as "The Organizer of Victory," was placed in charge of reorganizing the French army. The entire nation was conscripted into service (Levée en masse) as war was defined as a national mission.

The most notorious event of the French Revolution was the famous "Reign of Terror" (1793 – 1794), the government's campaign against its internal enemies and counterrevolutionaries. Revolutionary Tribunals were created to hear the cases of accused enemies brought to "justice" under a new Law of Suspects. Approximately 25,000 people throughout France lost their lives. Execution by guillotine became a spectator sport. A new political culture began to emerge, called the "Republic of Virtue." This was Robespierre's grand scheme to de-Christianize France and inculcate revolutionary virtue. The terror spiraled out of control, consuming leading Jacobin leaders (Danton, DesMoulins, and Hébert) until no one could feel secure in the shadow of Robespierre's dictatorship. On July 27, 1794 Robespierre was denounced in the Convention, arrested and executed the next day along with his close associate St. Just.

The fall of Robespierre was followed by a dramatic swing to the right called the Thermidorian Reaction (1794). Tired of terror and virtue alike, the moderate bourgeoisie politicians regained control of the National Convention. The Girondins were readmitted. A retreat from the excesses of revolution was begun. A new constitution was written in 1795, which set up a republican form of government. A new Legislative Assembly would choose a five-member executive, the Directory, from which the new regime was to take its name. Before its rule came to an end, the Convention removed all economic controls, which dealt a death blow to the Sans-culottes. Finally the Convention decreed that at least for the first two years of operation the new government reserve two-thirds of the seats in the Legislative Assembly for themselves.

1.5.4 *The Directory, 1795 – 1799*

The Constitution of 1795 set the tone and style of government in France: voting and holding office was reserved to property owners. The middle class was in control. They wanted peace in order to gain more wealth and to establish a society in which money and property would become the only requirements for prestige and power. These goals confronted opposition groups such as the aristocracy, who in October, 1795 attempted a royalist uprising. It might have succeeded were it not for the young Napoleon Bonaparte, who happened to be in Paris at the time and loyally helped the government put down the rebellion. The Sans-culottes repeatedly attacked the government and its economic philosophy, but leaderless and powerless they were doomed to failure. Despite growing inflation and mass public dissatisfaction, the Directory government ignored a growing shift in public opinion. When elections in April, 1797 produced a triumph for the royalist right the results were annulled and the Directory shed its last pretense of legitimacy.

Military success overshadowed the weak and corrupt Directory government. French armies annexed the Austrian Netherlands, the left bank of the Rhine, Nice and Savoy. The Dutch republic was made a satellite state of France. The greatest military victories were won by Napoleon Bonaparte, who drove the Austrians out of northern Italy and forced them to sign the Treaty of Campo Formio (October, 1797) in return for which the Directory government agreed to Bonaparte's scheme to conquer Egypt and threaten English interests in the East.

The Directory government managed to hang on for two more years, thanks to the military successes. But a steady loss of support continued in the face of a government that was bankrupt, filled with corruption and unwilling to halt an inflationary spiral that was aggravating the already impoverished masses of French peasants. The spirit of revolution was being crushed in the land, and this fear gave rise to a conspiracy to save the Revolution and forestall a royalist return to power. Led by the famous revolutionary, the Abbé Siéyès, Napoleon Bonaparte was invited to join the conspirators, which he did upon returning from Egypt. On November 9, 1799, they ousted the Directory. The conspirators quickly promulgated a new constitution which established the Consulate Era.

1.6   EVALUATION

1.6.1   *European Reaction to the Events of 1789 – 1799*

Liberals and radicals hailed the birth of liberty and freedom. Among those who explicitly defended the French Revolution were the German philosophers Immanuel Kant and Johann Fichte, the English scientist Joseph Priestly, and the American pamphleteer Tom Paine. Not all reaction was favorable. Conservatives predicted societal anarchy would ensue everywhere if the French revolutionaries succeeded. Friedrich Von Gentz and Edmund Burke, whose 1790 "Reflections on the Revolution in France" remains to this day as the classic statement of the conservative view of history. It was the romantic poet William Wordsworth who captured the sense of liberation and limitless hope inspired by the French Revolution:

> *"Bliss it was in that dawn to be alive*
> *But to be young was very heaven."*

1.6.2   *Results*

The first ten years of revolution in France destroyed the old social system and replaced it with a new one based on equality, ability and the law; guaranteed the triumph of capitalist society; gave birth to the notion of secular democracy; laid the foundations for the establishment of the modern nation-state; and gave the great mass of the human race what it had never had before except from religion: hope.

CHAPTER 2

THE FRENCH REVOLUTION II: THE ERA OF NAPOLEON, 1799–1815

After the first ten years of revolution, the shift to a new group in power in 1799 did not prepare anyone in France for the most dramatic changes that would distinguish this era from the previous changes of government of the past ten years. France was about to be mastered by a legendary "giant" and Europe overwhelmed by a mythical titan.

2.1   BACKGROUND OF NAPOLEON'S LIFE

Napoleon was born of Italian descent on the island of Corsica, August 15, 1769 to a prominent Corsican family one year after France annexed the island. He pursued a military career while advocating Corsican independence. He associated with Jacobins and advanced rapidly in the army when vacancies were caused by the emigration of aristocratic officers. His first marriage was to Josephine de Beauharnais, who was divorced by Napoleon after a childless marriage. In 1810 Napoleon arranged a marriage of state with Marie Louise, daughter of the Austrian emperor. Their son was known as Napoleon II, "King of Rome."

Napoleon was a military genius whose specialty was artillery. He was also a charismatic leader with the nationalist's clarity of mind and the romantic urge for action. Napoleon galvanized a dispirited, divided country into a unified and purposeful nation at the price of individual liberty.

2.2 ROLE IN DIRECTORY GOVERNMENT, 1795 – 1799

In 1793 Napoleon was responsible for breaking the British siege of Toulon. Because of his loyalty to the revolution, he was made Commander of the Army of the Interior after saving the new Directory government from being overthrown by a Parisian mob in 1795. He was selected to lead an army into Italy in the Campaign of 1796 against the First Coalition (1792 – 97) where he defeated the Austrians and Sardinians and imposed the Treaty of Campo Formio (1797) on Austria and effectively ended the First Coalition. England was thereby isolated.

The election results of 1797 forced the Directory government to abandon the wishes of the country and establish a dictatorship of those favorable to the revolution ("Post-Fructidorian Terror"). After defending the government, Napoleon launched his invasion of Egypt (1798), only to have his navy destroyed by England's Lord Nelson at the Battle of the Nile. Napoleon and the French army were isolated in North Africa.

Popular indignation against the Directory government, along with financial disorder and military losses, produced a crisis atmosphere in France. Fearing a return to monarchy, a group of conspirators headed by the Abbé Siéyès decided to save the revolution by overthrowing the Directory. Napoleon was invited to furnish the armed power and his popular name to the takeover (Coup d'État Brumaire, November 9, 1799).

2.3 CONSULATE PERIOD, 1799 – 1804 (ENLIGHTENED REFORM)

2.3.1 *Domestic Accomplishments*

The new government was installed on December 25, 1799 with a constitution which concentrated supreme power in the hands of Napoleon.

Executive power was vested in three consuls, but the First Consul (Napoleon) behaved more as an enlightened despot than revolutionary statesman. His aim was to govern France by demanding obedience, rewarding ability and organizing everything in orderly hierarchical fashion.

Napoleon's domestic reforms and policies affected every aspect of society and had an enduring impact on French history. Among the features were the following:

1) strong central government and administrative unity;

2) religious unity (Concordat of 1801 with the Roman Catholic Church);

3) financial unity (Bank of France), emphasizing balanced budget and rigid economy in government;

4) economic reform to stimulate the economy, provide food at low prices, increase employment and allowing peasants to keep the land they had secured during the revolution; and

5) educational reforms based on a system of public education under state control (University of France).

The Legal Unity provided the first clear and complete codification of French law (Code Napoleon) which made permanent many of the achievements of the French Revolution. It stipulated equality before the law, freedom of conscience, property rights, abolition of serfdom, and the secular character of the state. Its major regressive provisions denied women equal status with men, and denied true political liberty.

Thus, in the tradition of enlightened despotism, Napoleon repressed liberty, subverted republicanism and restored absolutism to France.

2.4 EMPIRE PERIOD, 1804 – 1814 (WAR AND DEFEAT)

2.4.1 Restoration of Monarchy

After being made Consul for Life (1801), Napoleon felt that only through an Empire could France retain its position and relate to other European states. On December 2, 1804, Napoleon crowned himself Emperor of France in Notre-Dame Cathedral.

2.4.2 Militarism and Empire Building

Beginning in 1805 Napoleon engaged in constant warfare that placed French troops in enemy capitals from Lisbon and Madrid to Berlin and Moscow, and temporarily gave Napoleon the largest empire since Roman times. Napoleon's Grand Empire consisted of an enlarged France and satellite kingdoms, as well as coerced allies.

The military campaigns of the Napoleonic Years included

the War of the Second Coalition (1798–1801), the War of the Third Coalition (1805 – 1807), the Peninsular War (1808 – 1814), the "War of Liberation" (1809), the Russian Campaign (1812), the War of the Fourth Coalition (1813 – 1814), and the Hundred Days (March 20 – June 22, 1815)

French-ruled subject peoples viewed Napoleon as a tyrant who repressed and exploited them for France's glory and advantage. Enlightened reformers believed Napoleon had betrayed the ideals of the Revolution.

The downfall of Napoleon resulted from the interaction of these events:

1) his inability to conquer England;

2) economic distress caused by the Continental System (boycott of British goods);

3) the Peninsular War with Spain;

4) the German War of Liberation; and

5) the Invasion of Russia

The actual defeat of Napoleon was the result of the Fourth Coalition and the Battle of Leipzig ("Battle of Nations"). Napoleon was exiled to the island of Elba as a sovereign with an income from France.

After learning of allied disharmony at the Vienna peace talks, Napoleon left Elba and began the "Hundred Days" by seizing power from the restored French king, Louis XVIII.

Napoleon's gamble ended at Waterloo in June 1815. He was now exiled as a prisoner of war to the South Atlantic island of St. Helena where he died in 1821.

2.5 EVALUATION

The significance of the Napoleonic era lies in the fact that it produced the first egalitarian dictatorship of modern times.

Although Napoleon ruled France for only fifteen years, his impact had lasting consequences on French and world history:

1) He consolidated revolutionary institutions.

2) He thoroughly centralized the French government.

3) He made a lasting settlement with the Church.

4) He spread the positive achievements of the French Revolution to the rest of the world.

Napoleon also repressed liberty, subverted republicanism, oppressed conquered peoples and caused terrible suffering.

The Napoleonic Legend, based on the personal memoirs of Napoleon, suggest an attempt by Napoleon to rewrite history by interpreting past events in a positive light.

EXTENT OF NAPOLEONIC POWER, 1812

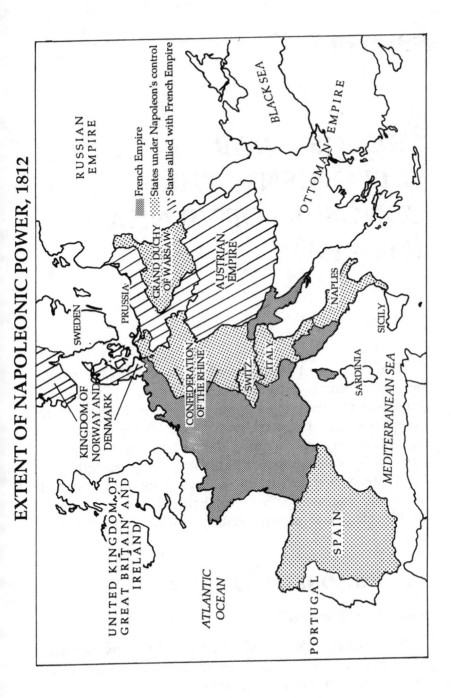

French Empire

States under Napoleon's control

States allied with French Empire

RUSSIAN EMPIRE

BLACK SEA

OTTOMAN EMPIRE

GRAND DUCHY OF WARSAW

PRUSSIA

AUSTRIAN EMPIRE

SWEDEN

KINGDOM OF NORWAY AND DENMARK

CONFEDERATION OF THE RHINE

SWITZ.

ITALY

NAPLES

SICILY

SARDINIA

UNITED KINGDOM OF GREAT BRITAIN AND IRELAND

ATLANTIC OCEAN

MEDITERRANEAN SEA

SPAIN

PORTUGAL

CHAPTER 3

THE POST-WAR SETTLEMENT: THE CONGRESS OF VIENNA, 1814 – 1815

The Congress of Vienna met in 1814 and 1815 to redraw the map of Europe after the Napoleonic era and to provide some way of preserving the future peace of Europe. While Europe was spared a general war throughout the remainder of the 19th century, the failure of the statesmen who shaped the future in 1814 – 1815 to recognize the forces unleashed by the French Revolution such as nationalism and liberalism only postponed the ultimate confrontation between two views of the world: change and accommodation or maintaining the status quo.

3.1 PERSONALITIES

3.1.1 *The "Big Four"*

The Vienna settlement was the work of the representatives of the four nations that had done the most to defeat Napoleon: England, Austria, Russia and Prussia.

Prince Klemens Von Metternich, who represented Austria, epitomized conservative reactionism. He resisted change, and was generally unfavorable to ideas of liberals and reformers because of the impact such forces would have on the multinational Hapsburg Empire.

Lord Castlereagh was England's representative. His principal objective was to achieve a balance of power on the continent by surrounding France with larger and stronger states.

Karl Von Hardenberg, as chancellor, represented Prussia. His goal was to recover Prussian territory lost to Napoleon in 1807 and gain additional territory in northern Germany (Saxony).

Czar Alexander I represented Russia. He was a mercurial figure who vacillated between liberal and reactionary views. The one specific "non-negotiable" goal he advanced was a "free" and "independent" Poland with himself as its king.

While Perigord Talleyrand, the French Foreign Minister, was not initially included in the early deliberations, he became a mediator where the interests of Prussia and Russia clashed with those of England and Austria. He thereby brought France into the ranks of the principal powers.

3.1.2 *The "Dancing Congress"*

This European gathering was held amid much pageantry. Parties, balls, and banquets reminded the delegates what life had been like before 1789. This was intended to generate favorable "public opinion" and occupy the delegates, since they had little to do of any serious nature.

3.2 PRINCIPLES OF SETTLEMENT: LEGITIMACY, COMPENSATION, BALANCE OF POWER

"Legitimacy" meant returning to power the ruling families deposed by more than two decades of revolutionary warfare. Bourbon rulers were restored in France, Spain and Naples. Dynasties were restored in Holland, Sardinia, Tuscany and Modena. Papal States were returned to the Pope.

"Compensation" meant territorially rewarding those states which had made considerable sacrifices to defeat Napoleon. England received far-flung naval bases (Malta, Ceylon, Cape of Good Hope). Austria recovered the Italian province of Lombardy and was awarded adjacent Venetia as well as Galicia (from Poland) and the Illyrian Provinces along the Adriatic. Russia was given most of Poland with the Czar as King, as well as Finland and Bessarabia. Prussia was awarded the Rhineland, three-fifths of Saxony and part of Poland. Sweden was given Norway.

"Balance of Power" meant arranging the map of Europe so that never again could one state (like France) upset the international order and cause a general war.

Encirclement of France was achieved through the following:

1) a strengthened Netherlands, by uniting Belgium (Austrian Netherlands) to Holland to form the Kingdom of the United Netherlands, a much larger state north of France;

2) Prussia receiving Rhenish lands bordering on the eastern French frontier;

3) Switzerland receiving a guarantee of perpetual neutrality;

4) enhancing Austrian influence over the Germanies by creating the German Confederation (Bund) of thirty-nine states with Austria designated as President of the Diet (Assembly) of the Confederation; and

5) Sardinia having its former territory restored, with the addition of Genoa.

3.3 ENFORCEMENT PROVISIONS (CONCERT OF EUROPE)

Arrangements to guarantee the enforcement of the status quo as defined by the Vienna settlement now included two provisions:

1) The "Holy Alliance" of Czar Alexander I of Russia, which was an idealistic and unpractical plan, existed only on paper. No one except Alexander took it seriously.

2) The "Quadruple Alliance" of Russia, Prussia, Austria and England provided for concerted action to arrest any threat to the peace or balance of power.

England defined concerted action as the great powers meeting in "Congress" to solve each problem as it arose so that no state would act unilaterally and independently of the other great powers. France was always believed to be the possible violator of the Vienna settlement.

Austria believed concerted action meant the great powers defending the status quo as established at Vienna against any change or threat to the system. Thus liberal or nationalist agitation was unhealthy for the body politic.

3.3.1 *Congress System*

From 1815 to 1822 European international relations were controlled by the series of meetings held by the great powers to monitor and defend the status quo: the Congress of Aix-la-Chapelle (1818); the Congress of Troppau (1820); the Congress of Laibach (1821); and the Congress of Verona (1822).

The principle of collective security required unanimity among members of the Quadruple Alliance. The history of the Congress System points to the ultimate failure of this key provision in light of the serious challenges to the status quo after 1815 (See Chapter 6).

3.4 EVALUATION

The Congress of Vienna has been criticized for ignoring the liberal and nationalist aspirations of so many peoples. Hindsight suggests the statesmen at Vienna may have been more successful in stabilizing the international system than we have been able to do in the 20th century. Not until the unification of Germany in 1870 – 71 was the balance of power upset; not until World War I in 1914 did Europe have another general war. But hindsight also instructs us that the leading statesmen at Vienna underestimated the new nationalism generated by the French Revolution, that they did not understand the change that citizen armies and national wars had effected among people in their attitude toward political problems. The men at Vienna in 1815 underestimated the growing liberalism of the age and failed to see that an industrial revolution was beginning to create a new alignment of social classes and create new needs and issues.

EUROPE 1815 (After the Congress of Vienna)

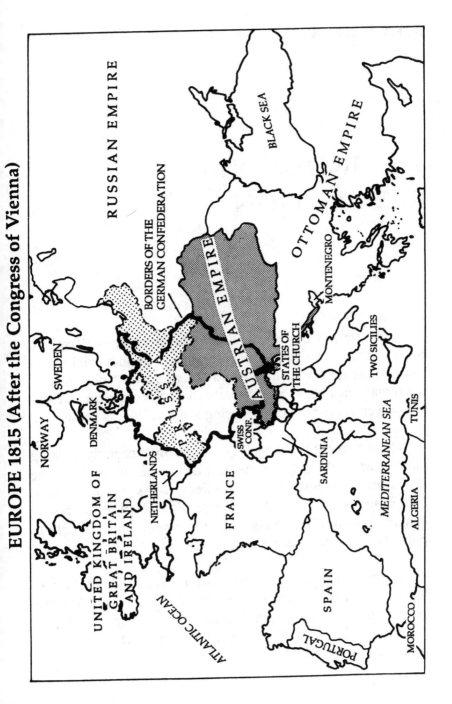

CHAPTER 4

THE INDUSTRIAL REVOLUTION

In the late 19th century the English historian Arnold Toynbee began to refer to the period since 1750 as "The Industrial Revolution." The term was intended to describe a time of transition when machines began significantly to displace human and animal power in methods of producing and distributing goods.

These changes began slowly, almost imperceptibly, gaining momentum with each decade so that by the midpoint of the 19th century, industrialism had swept across Europe west to east, from England to eastern Europe. Few countries purposely avoided industrialization because of its promise of material improvement and national wealth.

The economic changes that constitute the "Industrial Revolution" have done more than any other movement in Western civilization to revolutionize Western life by imparting to our cultures a uniqueness which never before, or perhaps since, has been matched or duplicated.

4.1 ENGLAND BEGINS THE REVOLUTION IN ENERGY AND INDUSTRY

Essentially, the "Industrial Revolution" describes a process of economic change from an agricultural and commercial society into a modern industrial society. This was a gradual process, where economic, social and political changes nonetheless produced a veritable revolution which Arnold Toynbee was the first to identify. He placed the origins of this remarkable transition in England.

Roots of the Industrial Revolution could be found in the following:

1) the Commercial Revolution (1500 – 1700), which spurred the great economic growth of Europe brought about by the Age of Discovery and Exploration, which in turn helped to solidify the economic doctrines of mercantilism;

2) the effect of the Scientific Revolution, which produced the first wave of mechanical inventions and technological advances;

3) the increase in population in Europe from 140 million people in 1750 to 266 million people by the mid-part of the 19th century (more producers, more consumers); and

4) the political and social revolutions of the 19th century, which began the rise to power of the "middle class", which provided leadership for the economic revolution.

England began the economic transformation by employing her unique assets:

1) a supply of cheap labor, as the result of the enclosure movement which created unemployment among the farmers (yeomen). Those former agricultural laborers were now available for hire in the new industrial towns;

2) a good supply of coal and iron, both indispensable for the technological and energy development of the "revolution";

3) the availability of large supplies of capital from profitable commercial activity in the preceding centuries ready to be invested in new enterprises;

4) a class of inventive people who possessed technological skill and whose independence and non-conformity allowed them to take risks;

5) as a colonial and maritime power, England had access to the raw materials needed for the development of many industries;

6) England had a government which was sympathetic to industrial development and well-established financial institutions ready to make loans available; and

7) after a long series of successful wars, England was undevastated and free to develop its new industries which prospered because of the economic dislocations caused by the Napoleonic Wars.

4.1.1 Early Progress

The revolution occurred first in the cotton and metallurgical industries, because those industries lent themselves to mechanization.

A series of mechanical inventions beginning in 1733 and lasting until 1793 would enable the cotton industry to mass-produce quality goods.

The need to replace wood as an energy source led to the use of coal which increased coal mining and resulted ultimately in the invention of the steam engine and the locomotive as inventions which sought to solve practical problems.

The development of steam power allowed the cotton industry to expand and transformed the iron industry. The factory system which had been created in response to the new energy sources and machinery was perfected to increase the amount of manufactured goods.

A transportation revolution ensued, in order to distribute the productivity of machinery as well as deliver raw materials to the eager factories. This led to the growth of canal systems, the construction of hard-surfaced "macadam" roads, the commercial use of the steamboat demonstrated by Robert Fulton, and the railway locomotive made commercially successful by George Stephenson.

Subsequent revolution in agriculture made it possible for fewer people to feed humankind, thus freeing people to work in factories or in the many new fields of communications, distribution of goods, or services like teaching, medicine and entertainment.

4.2 SPREAD OF INDUSTRIALIZATION TO EUROPE AND THE WORLD

During the first fifty years of the 19th century, industrialism swept across Europe west to east, from England to eastern Europe. In its wake all modes of life would be challenged and transformed.

4.2.1 *The Challenges to the Spread of Industrialism*

Continental economic growth had been retarded by the wars of the Napoleonic period.

Because England was so technically advanced European countries found it difficult to compete. However, catching up to England was made easy by avoiding the costly mistakes of early British experiments and using the power of strong central governments and banking systems to promote native industry. But on the continent there was no large labor supply in cities; iron and coal deposits were not as concentrated as in England.

4.2.2 *Route of Industrialization*

England was the undisputed economic and industrial leader until the mid-19th century. The industrialization of the continent occurred mostly in the latter half of the 19th century, and, in the southern and eastern regions, in the 20th century.

By 1830 industrialism had begun to spread from England to Belgium, France and other scattered areas of Europe. These successful industrial operations were due to the exportation from England of machines, management and capital. Germany was slower in following English methods until a tariff policy was established in 1834 (the *Zollverein*) which induced capital investment in German manufacturers.

4.3 GROWTH OF INDUSTRIAL SOCIETY

The undermining and eventual elimination of Western society's traditional social stratification model (i.e., clergy, nobility and the masses) would be the result of the Industrial Revolution.

4.3.1 The Bourgeoisie: The New Aristocracy

The middle class were the major contributors as well as the principal beneficiaries of early industrialism. They measured success in monetary terms and most tended to be indifferent to the human suffering of the new wage-earning class. The industrial bourgeoisie had two levels: 1) upper bourgeoisie, i.e., great bankers, merchants and industrialists who demanded free enterprise and high tariffs; and, 2) lower bourgeoisie, i.e., small industrialists, merchants and professional men who demanded stability and security from government.

4.3.2 The Factory Worker: The New Wage-Earning Class

The Industrial Revolution created a unique new category of people who were dependent on their job alone for income, a job from which they might be dismissed without cause. The factory worker had no land, no home, no source of income but his job. During the first century of the Industrial Revolution the factory worker was completely at the mercy of the law of supply and demand for labor.

Working in the factory meant more self-discipline and less personal freedom for workers. The system tended to depersonalize society and reduced workers to an impersonal status. The statistics with regard to wages, diet, and clothing suggest overall improvement for the workers, with some qualifications, since some industries were notoriously guilty of social injustices. Contemporary social critics complained that industrialism brought misery to the workers while others claimed life was improving. Until 1850 workers as a whole did not share in the general wealth produced by the Industrial Revolution. Conditions would improve as the century wore on, as union action combined with general prosperity and a developing social conscience to improve the working conditions, wages, and hours first of skilled labor and later of unskilled labor.

4.4 SOCIAL EFFECTS OF INDUSTRIALIZATION

The most important sociological result of industrialism was the urbanization of the world. The new factories acted as a magnet pulling people away from their rural roots and beginning the most massive population transfer in history. Thus the birth of factory towns and cities that grew into large industrial centers.

The role of the city changed in the 19th century from governmental and cultural centers to industrial centers with all the problems of urbanization.

Workers in cities became aware of their numbers and their common problems, so cities made the working class a powerful force by raising their consciousness and enabling them to unite for political action to remedy their economic dissatisfaction.

It is in this urban setting that the century's great social and political dilemmas were framed: working class injustices, gender exploitation and standard-of-living issues.

Family structure and gender roles within the family were altered by the growth of industrialism. Families as an economic unit were no longer the chief unit of both production and consumption but rather consumption alone.

New wage economy meant that families were less closely bound together than in the past; the economic link was broken. Productive work was taken out of the home (cottage) and placed elsewhere. As factory wages for skilled adult males rose, women and children were separated from the workplace. A new pattern of family life emerged.

Gender-determined roles in the home and domestic life emerged slowly. Married women came to be associated with domestic duties while the male tended to be the sole wage earner.

Single women and widows had much work available, but that work commanded low wages and low skills and provided no way to protect themselves from exploitation.

Marriage as an institution in the wage economy began to change. Women were now expected to create a nurturing environment to which the family members returned after work. Married women worked outside the home only when family needs, illness or death of a spouse required them to do so.

4.5 EVALUATION

The Industrial Revolution conquered and harnessed the forces of nature: water power, coal, oil, and electricity all provided power to replace human effort. The amount of wealth available for human consumption increased. Vast amounts of food, clothing and energy were produced and distributed to the workers of the world. Luxuries were made commonplace, life expectancy increased and leisure time made more enjoyable.

But the workers would not begin to share in this dramatic increase in the standard of living until the second half of the 19th century when all the evils associated with the factory system (low wages, poor working conditions, etc.) and early industrialism in general were corrected. In the first century of industrialism the wealth created went almost exclusively to the entrepreneur and the owner of capital—the middle class.

CHAPTER 5

IMPACT OF THOUGHT SYSTEMS (ISMS) ON THE EUROPEAN WORLD

Ideologies

The mind set of Western civilization was being challenged in the first half of the 19th century by the appearance of numerous new thought systems. Not since the 18th century Enlightenment had humans sought to catalog, classify and categorize their thoughts and beliefs. Several of these systems of thought acted as change agents throughout the 19th century, while others would flow into the 20th century and continue to define the modern world.

5.1   ROMANTICISM

Romanticism was a reaction against the rigid classicism, rationalism and deism of the 18th century. Strongest in application between 1800 and 1850, the romantic movement differed from country to country and from romanticist to romanticist. Because it emphasized change it was considered revolutionary in all aspects of life. It was an atmosphere in which events occurred and came to affect not only the way humans thought and expressed themselves but also the way they lived socially and politically.

5.1.1 Characteristics

Romanticism appealed to emotion rather than to reason (i.e., truth and virtue can be found just as surely by the heart rather than the head), and rejected classical emphasis on order and the observance of rules (i.e., let the imagination create new cultural forms and techniques).

It also rejected the enlightenment view of nature as a precise harmonious whole (i.e., viewed nature as alive, vital, changing and filled with the divine spirit), as well as the cold impersonal religion of Deism (i.e., viewed God as inspiring human nobility; deplored decline of Christianity).

Romanticism further rejected the Enlightenment point of view of the past which was counter-progressive to human history (i.e., viewed the world as an organism that was growing and changing with each nation's history unique), and expressed vital optimism about life and the future.

Romantics enriched European cultural life by encouraging personal freedom and flexibility. By emphasizing feeling, humanitarian movements were created to fight slavery, poverty and industrial evils.

5.1.2 Romantic Literature, Art, Music, and Philosophy

English romantics like Wordsworth and Coleridge epitomized the romantic movement, along with Burns, Byron, Shelley, Keats, Tennyson, Browning and Scott. The greatest German figures were Goethe, Schiller, Heine and Herder. French romantics were Hugo, Balzac, Dumas and Stendahl. The outstanding Russian exponents were Pushkin, Dostoevski and Turgenev. Among the greatest American figures were Longfellow, Cooper, Irving, Emerson, Poe, Whitman and Thoreau.

The leading romantic painters in popular taste were the Frenchmen Millet and David, the Englishmen Turner and Constable, and the Spaniard Goya. Gothic Revival Style marked the Romantic era in architecture.

Music did not change as dramatically as did literature. Classical forms were still observed but new ideas and innovations were increasing. Beethoven was a crossover while straight romantics would include Brahms, Schumann, Schubert, Berlioz, Chopin and Von Weber.

Romantic philosophy stimulated an interest in Idealism, the belief that reality consists of ideas, as opposed to materialism. This school of thought (Philosophical Idealism) founded by Plato was developed through the writings of 1) Immanuel Kant whose work, *Critique of Pure Reason*, advances the theory that reality was two-fold — physical and spiritual. Reason can discover what is true in the physical but not in the spiritual world; 2) Johann Gottlieb Fichte, a disciple of Kant, and Friedrich Schelling, collaborator of Fichte; and, 3) Georg Wilhelm Hegel, the greatest exponent of this school of thought. Hegel believed that an impersonal God rules the universe and guides humans along a progressive evolutionary course by means of process called dialecticism; this is an historical process by which one thing is constantly reacting with its opposite (the thesis and antithesis) producing a result (synthesis) that automatically meets another opposite and continues the series of reactions. Hegel's philosophy exerted a great influence over Karl Marx who turned the Hegelian dialectic upside down to demonstrate the ultimate meaning of reality was a material end, not a higher or spiritual end as Hegel suggested.

5.1.3 *Impact*

Romanticism destroyed the clear simplicity and unity of thought which characterized the 18th century. There was no longer one philosophy which expressed all the aims and ideals of Western civilization. Romanticism provided a more complex but truer view of the real world.

5.2 CONSERVATISM

Conservatism arose in reaction to liberalism and became a popular alternative for those who were frightened by the violence, terror and social disorder unleashed by the French Revolution. Early conservatism was allied to the restored monarchical governments of Austria, Russia, France and England. Support for conservatism came from the traditional ruling classes, as well as the peasants who still formed the majority of the population. Intellectual ammunition came from the pens of the Englishman Edmund Burke; the Frenchmen, Joseph de Maistre and Louis de Bonald; the Austrian Friedrich Gentz; and many of the early romantics. In essence, conservatives believed in order, society and the state; faith and tradition.

5.2.1 *Characteristics*

Conservatives viewed history as a continuum which no single generation can revoke.

Conservatives believed the basis of society was organic not contractual. Society was not a machine with replaceable parts. Stability and longevity, not progress and change, mark a good society.

The only legitimate sources of political authority were God and history. The social contract theory was rejected because a contract cannot make authority legitimate.

Investing society with the theory of individualism ignored humans as social beings and undermined the concept of community which was essential to life. Conservatives said self-interest does not lead to social harmony but to social conflict.

Conservatives argued that measuring happiness and progress in material terms ignored humans as spiritual beings.

Conservatives rejected the philosophy of natural rights and believed that rights did not pertain to people everywhere but were determined and allocated by a particular state.

With its exaggerated emphasis on reason and intellect the conservatives denounced the philosophes and reformers for ignoring each human as an emotional being and underestimating the complexity of human nature.

To conservatives, society was hierarchical, i.e., some humans were better able to rule and lead than those who were denied intelligence, education, wealth and birth.

5.2.2 *Impact*

Conservatism was basically "anti-" in its propositions. It never had a feasible program of its own. The object of their hatred was a liberal society which they claimed was antisocial and morally degrading. While their criticisms contained much justification, conservatives ignored the positive and promising features of liberal society. Conservative criticism did poke holes in liberal ideology and pointed toward a new social tyranny, the aggressive middle class.

5.3 LIBERALISM

The theory of liberalism was the first major theory in the history of Western thought to teach that the individual is a self-sufficient being whose freedom and well-being are the sole reasons for the existence of society. Liberalism was more closely connected to the spirit and outlook of the enlightenment than any of the other "isms" of the early 19th century. While the general principles and attitudes associated with liberalism varied considerably from country to country, liberals tended to come from the middle class or bourgeoisie and favored increased liberty for their class and indirectly for the masses of people, as long as the latter did not in their turn ask for so much freedom that they endangered the security of the middle class. Liberalism was reformist and political rather than revolutionary in character.

5.3.1 Characteristics

Individuals are entitled to seek their freedom in the face of arbitrary or tyrannical restrictions imposed upon them.

Humans have certain natural rights and governments should protect them. These rights include the right to own property, freedom of speech, freedom from excessive punishment, freedom of worship, and freedom of assembly.

These rights are best guaranteed by a written constitution with careful definition of the limits to which governmental actions may go. Examples include the American Declaration of Independence (1776) and the French Declaration of Rights of man (1789).

Another view of liberalism was presented by individuals who came to be known as the utilitarians. Their founder, Jeremy Bentham, held the pleasure-pain principle as the key idea – that humans are ordained to avoid pain and to seek pleasure.

Bentham equated pleasure with good and pain with evil. The goodness or badness of any act, individual or public, was found by balancing the pleasure against the pain it caused. Thus one came to test the utility of any proposed law or institution, i.e., "the greatest happiness of the greatest number."

Liberals advocated economic individualism (i.e., laissez-faire capitalism) heralded by Adam Smith in his 1776 economic masterpiece, *Wealth of Nations*. They regarded free enterprise as the most productive economy and the one that allowed for the greatest measure of individual choice.

Economic inequality will exist and is acceptable, liberals held, because it does not detract from the individual's moral dignity nor does it conflict with equality of opportunity and equality before the law.

Economic liberalism claimed to be based on the realities of a new industrial era. The "classical economists" (Thomas Malthus and David Ricardo) taught that there were inescapable forces at work – competition, the pressure of population growth, the iron law of wages, and the law of supply and demand – in accordance with which economic life must function. It was the duty of government to remove any obstacle to the smooth operation of these natural forces.

Internationally, liberals believed in the balance-of-power system and free trade because each track allowed individual nations the opportunity to determine its own course of action.

Liberals believed in the pluralistic society as long as it did not block progress. War and revolutionary change disrupt progress and enlarge the power of government.

Education was an indispensable prerequisite to individual responsibility and self-government.

5.3.2 Early Nineteenth Century Advocates of Liberalism

In England, advocates included the political economists, the utilitarians and individuals like Thomas Robington Macaulay and John Stuart Mill; in France, Benjamin Constant, Victor Cousin, Jean Baptiste Say and Alexis de Tocqueville; in Germany, Wilhelm von Humboldt, Friedrich List, Karl von Rotteck and Karl Theodor Welcker.

5.3.3 Impact

Liberalism was involved in the various revolutionary movements of the early 19th century (see Chapters 6 and 7). It found concrete expression in over ten constitutions secured between 1815 and 1848 in states of the German Confederation. Its power was demonstrated in the reform measures which successive British governments adopted during these same decades. It affected German student organizations and permeated Prussian life.

Alexis de Toqueville spoke for many liberals when he warned against the masses' passion for equality and their willingness to sacrifice political liberty in order to improve their material well-being. These fears were not without foundation. In the 20th century, the masses have sometimes shown themselves willing to trade freedom for authority, order, economic security and national power.

5.4 NATIONALISM

The regenerative force of liberal thought in early 19th century Europe was dramatically revealed in the explosive force of the power of nationalism. Raising the level of consciousness of people having a common language, a common soil, common traditions, a common history, a common culture and a shared human experience to seek political unity around an identity of what or who constitutes the nation was aroused and made militant during the turbulent French Revolutionary era.

5.4.1 Characteristics

Early nationalist sentiment was romantic, exuberant and cosmopolitan as compared to the more intense, hate-filled nationalism of the latter half of the 19th century.

The breakdown of society's traditional loyalties to church, dynastic state and region began during the course of the 18th century. Impelled by the French Revolutionary dogma, new loyalties were fashioned — that people possessed the supreme power (sovereignty) of the nation and were, therefore, the true nation united by common language, culture, history, etc. Only then would people develop the sense of pride, tradition and common purpose which would come to characterize modern nationalism.

Nationalism, as loyalty to one's nation, did not originate in the early 19th century. Men and women have been fighting for, and living and dying for their respective countries for hundreds of years. It wasn't until the early 19th century that this feeling and motivation changed into something far more intense and far more demanding than it had been. The focus of the loyalty changed from dynastic self-interest to individual self-interest as part of a greater collective consciousness.

5.4.2 Impact of Nationalism

Nationalistic thinkers and writers examined the language, literature and folkways of their people and thereby stimulated nationalist feelings. Emphasizing the history and culture of the various European peoples tended to reinforce and glorify national sentiment.

Most early 19th century nationalist leaders adopted the ideas of the German philosopher-historian Johann Gottfried Herder (1744 – 1803), who is regarded as the father of modern nationalism.

Herder taught that every people is unique and possesses a distinct national character, or *Volksgeist*, which has evolved over many centuries. No one culture or people is superior to any other. All national groups are parts of that greater whole which is humanity.

Herder's doctrine of the indestructible *Volksgeist* led to a belief that every nation has the right to become a sovereign state encompassing all members of the same nationality. Since most Western states contained people of many different nationalities, and few states contained all the members of any one nationality, nationalism came to imply the overthrow of almost every existing government.

5.4.3 Evaluation

Because of its inherently revolutionary implications, nationalism was suppressed by the established authorities. Yet it flourished in Germany where conservative and reactionary nationalists competed with a somewhat more liberal form of nationalism associated with intellectuals like Fichte, Hegel, Humboldt and Von Ranke. In Eastern Europe, conservative nationalists stressed the value of their own unique customs, culture and folkways, while Western European nationalists demanded liberal political reforms. The influence of the Italian Nationalist Mazzini and the Frenchman Michelet in stimulating nationalist feeling in the West was a key ingredient.

It should be noted that there was always a fundamental conflict between liberalism and nationalism. Liberals were rationalists who demanded objectivity in studying society and history while nationalists relied on emotion and would do anything to exalt the nation, even subvert individual rights. By the late 19th century nationalism was promoting competition and warfare between peoples and threatened to douse liberal ideas of reason and freedom.

5.5 SOCIALISM

With the chief beneficiaries of industrialism being the new middle class, the increasing misery of the working classes disturbed the conscience of concerned liberal thinkers (Bentham and Mill) who proposed a modification of the concept of laissez-faire economics. Other socially concerned thinkers observing the injustices and inefficiencies of capitalistic society began to define the social question in terms of human equality and the means to be followed in order to secure this goal. As cures for the social evils of industrialism were laid out in elaborate detail, the emerging dogma came to be called socialism.

5.5.1 *Characteristics*

Since biblical times humans have been concerned with the problem of social justice, but it was not until the 19th century that it possessed a broader intellectual base and a greater popular support than it had ever enjoyed in the past. The difficulty with the existing system, according to social critics of the day, was that it permitted wealth to be concentrated in the hands of a small group of persons and deprived the working classes of a just share in what was rightfully theirs. A social mechanism had to be developed so a just distribution of society's wealth could be attained. The result was a variety of approaches.

The Utopian Socialists (from *Utopia*, Saint Thomas More's book on a fictional ideal society) were the earliest writers to propose an equitable solution to improve the distribution of society's wealth. While they endorsed the productive capacity of industrialism they denounced its mismanagement. Human society was to be organized as a community rather than a mixture of competing selfish individuals. All the goods a person needed could be produced in one community.

Generally, the utopians advocated some kind of harmonious society, some form of model communities, social workshops or the like, where the ruthless qualities of an individualistic capitalism would disappear.

Utopian ideas were generally regarded as idealistic and visionary with no practical application. With little popular support from either the political establishment or the working classes, the movement failed to produce any substantial solution to the social question. Leading Utopian thinkers included Henri de Saint-Simon (1760 – 1825), Charles Fourier (1772 – 1837), Robert Owen (1771 – 1858), and Louis Blanc (1811 – 1882).

The Anarchists rejected industrialism and the dominance of government. Auguste Blanqui (1805 – 1881) advocated terrorism as a means to end capitalism and the state. Pierre Joseph Proudhon (1809 – 1865) attacked the principle of private property because it denied justice to the common people.

Christian Socialism began in England circa 1848. Believing that the evils of industrialism would be ended by following Christian principles, the advocates of this doctrine tried to bridge the gap between the anti-religious drift of socialism and the need for Christian social justice for workers. The best-known Christian Socialist was the novelist Charles Kingsley (1814 – 1875), whose writings exposed the social evils of industrialism.

"Scientific" Socialism, or Marxism, was the creation of Karl Marx (1818 – 1883), a German scholar who, with the help of Friedrich Engels (1820 – 1895), intended to replace utopian hopes and dreams with a brutal, militant blueprint for socialist working class success. The principal works of this revolutionary school of socialism were *The Communist Manifesto* and *Das Kapital (Capital)*.

The theory of Dialectical Materialism enabled Marx to explain the history of the world. By borrowing Hegel's dialectic, substituting materialism and realism in place of Hegel's idealism and inverting the methodological process, Marx was able to justify his theoretical conclusions.

Marxism consisted of a number of key propositions:

1) The economic interpretation of history, i.e., all human history has been determined by economic factors (mainly who controls the means of production and distribution).

2) The class struggle, i.e., since the beginning of time there has been a class struggle between the rich and the poor or the exploiters and the exploited.

3) Theory of Surplus Value, i.e., the true value of a product was labor and, since the worker received a small portion of his just labor price, the difference was surplus value, "stolen" from him by the capitalist.

4) Socialism was inevitable, i.e., capitalism contained the seeds of its own destruction (overproduction, unemployment, etc.); the rich will grow richer and the poor will grow poorer until the gap between each class (proletariat and bourgeoisie) is so great that the working classes will rise up in revolution and overthrow the elite bourgeoisie to install a "dictatorship of the proletariat". As modern capitalism is dismantled the creation of a classless society guided by the principle "From each accord-

ing to his abilities, to each according to his needs" will take place.

5.6   EVALUATION

Ideologies (isms) are interpretations of the world from a particular viewpoint. They are or imply programs of action and thrive where belief in general standards and norms has broken down. The proliferation of so many thought systems and movements based on them after 1815 suggest the basic division of society was between those who accepted the implications of the intellectual, economic, and political revolutions of the 18th and early 19th centuries and those who did not. The polarization in ideology was the result.

CHAPTER 6

EUROPE IN CRISIS, 1815 – 1833: REPRESSION, REFORM AND REVOLUTION

The Vienna peace settlement signaled the triumph of the political and social conservative order in Europe. The dangerous ideas (Liberalism and Nationalism) associated with the French Revolution and Napoleonic period had been "contained" by the territorial provisions of the 1815 agreement. The status quo had been once again defined. "Order" and "stability" was expected in the European state system.

Underestimating the power of ideas, the Conservative leadership after 1815 was instead faced with a dramatic confrontation between those who had been converted to the "new" ideas (which required political changes) and the traditional ruling classes, who were reluctant to make any accommodation with the believers in the "new" ideas. The result of such confrontation in most states was government-sponsored repression followed by revolution. Few states chose to respond to the call for liberal reform. Only nationalist impulses in Greece and Belgium were successful for reasons which could hardly comfort liberals. The intellectual climate of Romanticism provided a volatile atmosphere in which these events unfolded.

6.1   POST-WAR REPRESSION, 1815 – 1820

Initially the great powers followed the lead of the Austrian statesman Prince Metternich (1773 – 1859) in suppressing any direct or indirect expression of liberal faith. Most leaders attempted to reinstitute conservative means of governmental control in order to prevent reforms in the direction of greater participation by more people in government. The literate middle class, supported by urban workers, demanded reform and were willing to use violence to obtain it.

6.1.1   *England*

The Tory (Conservative) government which defeated Napoleon was in control of England. Facing serious economic problems which had produced large numbers of industrial unemployed, the conservatives tried to follow a reactionary policy:

1) The Corn Law of 1815 effectively halted the importation of cheaper foreign grains, aiding the Tory landholding aristocracy but increasing the cost of bread and driving the poor and unemployed to protest and demand parliamentary reform.

2) The Coercion Acts of 1817 suspended "habeas corpus" for the first time in English history; provided for arbitrary arrest and punishment; and drastically curtailed freedom of the press and public mass meetings.

3) The "Peterloo Massacre" of 1819 where several members of a large crowd listening to reformers demanding repeal of the Corn Laws and other liberal changes were

killed and hundreds injured when police authorities broke up the meeting.

4) The Six Acts of Parliament in 1819 in response to the "Peterloo" episode were a series of repressive measures which attempted to remove the instruments of agitation from the hands of radical leaders and to provide the authorities with new powers.

5) The Cato Street Conspiracy of 1820 when a group of extreme radicals plotted to blow up the entire British cabinet. Provided new support for repression by the Tories as well as discrediting the movement for parliamentary reform.

By 1820 England was on the road to becoming a reactionary authoritative state when numerous protests among younger Tories argued that such repressive legislation was not in the English tradition and that the party itself may need to change its direction.

6.1.2 France

France emerged from the chaos of the long revolutionary period (1789 – 1815) as the most liberal large state on the continent. The period from 1815 – 1830 is always referred to as the Restoration era signifying the return of the legitimate royal dynasty of France — the infamous Bourbon line.

Louis XVIII (reign 1814 – 1824) governed France as a Constitutional Monarch by agreeing to observe the "Charter" or Constitution of the Restoration Period. This moderate document managed to limit royal power, grant legislative powers, protect civil rights, uphold the Code Napoleon and other pre-restoration reforms.

Louis XVIII wished to unify the French populace, which was divided into those who accepted the Revolution and those who did not. The leader of those who did not was the Count of Artois (1757 – 1836), brother of the king and leader of the Ultra Royalists.

The 1815 "White Terror" saw royalist mobs murder thousands of former revolutionaries.

New elections in 1816 for the Chamber of Deputies resulted in the Ultras being rejected in favor of a moderate royalist majority dependent on middle class support. The war indemnity was paid off, France was admitted to the Quadruple Alliance (1818) and liberal sentiment began to grow.

In February 1820 the Duke of Berri, son of Artois and heir to the throne after his father, was murdered. Royalists charged the left (Liberals) were responsible and that the king's policy of moderation had encouraged the left.

Louis XVIII began to move the government more and more to the right as changes in the electoral laws narrowed the eligible voters to the most wealthy and censorship was imposed. Liberals were being driven out of legal political life and into near-illegal activity. The triumph of reactionism came in 1823 when French troops were authorized by the Concert of Europe to crush the Spanish Revolution and restore another Bourbon ruler, Ferdinand VII.

6.1.3 Austria and the German States

Throughout the first half of the 19th century the Austrian Empire and the German Confederation were dominated by Prince Metternich, who epitomized conservative reactionism. To no other country or empire were the programs of liberalism and nationalism potentially more dangerous. Given the multiethnic composition of the Hapsburg empire any recognition of the political rights and aspirations of any of the national groups would mean the probable dissolution of the empire.

It was Napoleon who reduced over 300 German states to 39, and the Congress of Vienna which preserved this arrangement under Austrian domination. The purpose of the German confederation (Bund) was to guarantee the independence of the member states, and by joint action to preserve all German states from domestic disorder or revolution. Its organization of government was a Diet (assembly) presided over by Austria as President.

The two largest states in the confederation were Austria and Prussia. Austria was ruled by the Hapsburg dynasty and through Metternich's anti-liberal and nationalist pathology held the line against any change in the status quo.

Prussia was ruled by the Hohenzollern dynasty, a very aggressive royal family when it came to expanding the borders of this northern German state, sometimes at the expense of other German rulers. For a short time after 1815 German liberals looked to Prussia as a leader of German liberalism because of liberal reforms in government enacted after a humiliating defeat at the hands of Napoleon. These reforms were intended to improve the efficiency of government and were not the portent of a general trend. The Prussian government and its traditional ruling classes (Junkers) intended to follow the lead of Metternich in repressing all liberal-nationalist agitation.

Liberal-nationalist agitation was highly vocal and visible in and among German universities in the first half of the 19th century. Student organizations such as the Burschenschaften were openly promoting political arrangements which seemed radical and revolutionary at the time.

At the Wartbug Festival (1817), students burned various symbols of authority. Russian agent Kotzebue was assassinated in 1819 by Karl Sand, a student member of the Burschenschaften.

The Carlsbad Diet (1819) was summoned by Metternich to end the seditious activity of German liberals and nationalists. The passage of a series of decrees effectively ended the activities of these change-agents. In fact, the movement was driven underground.

6.1.4 Russia

From 1801 to 1825 Czar Alexander I governed this traditional authoritarian state. A man of many moods, this Russian emperor thought he was called upon to lead Europe into a new age of benevolence and good will. After the Congress of Vienna he became increasingly reactionary and a follower of Metternich.

Alexander I was torn between an intellectual attraction to the ideas of the Enlightenment and reform and a very pragmatic adherence to traditional Russian autocracy (absolutism).

With the help of liberal adviser Michael Speransky plans were made for a reconstruction of the Russian government because of the czar's admiration for Napoleon's administrative genius. This and other liberal policies alienated the nobility and Speransky was dismissed.

Alexander I came to regard the Enlightenment, the French Revolution and Napoleon in biblical terms, seeing all three as anti-Christian. Turning to a new reactionary advisor, General Arakcheiev, repression became the order of the day. There could be no toleration of political opposition or criticism of the regime. The early years of possible liberal reform had given way to conservative repression.

6.2   REVOLUTIONS I, 1820 – 1829

Nationalism, liberalism and industrialism were all key factors in the outbreak of revolution during the first half of the 19th century. All three "isms" were opposed by conservatives —including royalists, clergy, and the landed aristocracy—who were rooted in the way of life before the French Revolution. Promoting the new forces of change was a younger generation, the heirs of the Enlightenment who believed in progress. Romanticism was the backdrop against which these events were played out.

6.2.1   *The International System: The Concert of Europe*

At the 1815 Congress of Vienna the enforcement provisions of the settlement were designed to guarantee stability and peace in the international arena. The Quadruple Alliance (Austria, Russia, Prussia, England) that had defeated Napoleon was to continue through a new spirit of cooperation and consultation that would be referred to as the "Concert of Europe." At the suggestion of Lord Castlereagh, England's Foreign Minister, foreign policy issues affecting the international order would be worked out in a series of meetings or Congresses so that no one nation could act without the consent of the others. But under the leadership of Metternich, the Congress system became the means to preserve the political status quo of autocracy in Europe against all revolutionary ideas. The Congress system was short-lived because the continental powers could not always agree on cooperative action and the English refused to support interference in the domestic affairs of nation-states. In the end each nation became guided by its own best interests.

The Congress System of Conferences. The Congress of Aix-la-Chapelle (1818) arranged for the withdrawal of the allied army of occupation from France and the admission of France into the concert of Europe (Quintuple Alliance).

The Congress of Troppau (1820) was summoned by Metternich because of the outbreak of revolution in Spain. A policy statement (Protocol of Troppau) which would authorize armed intervention into any state which undergoes revolutionary change was opposed by England.

The Congress of Laibach (1821) authorized Austrian troops to end the revolutionary changes in the Kingdom of the Two Sicilies where revolutions had spread from Spain. No decision was made concerning Spain.

The Congress of Verona (1822) was called because of the continuing Spanish Revolution and the outbreak (1821) of revolution in Greece. When Russia, Prussia and Austria agreed to support French intervention in Spain, the new English Foreign Minister, George Canning (1770 – 1827) (Viscount Castlereagh had committed suicide) withdrew England from the Concert of Europe. Verona marked the effective end of the Congress system.

The Monroe Doctrine and the Concert of Europe. British fears that Metternich would attempt the restoration of Spain's colonies then revolting in Latin America prompted George Canning to suggest and then support the foreign policy statement of the United States of America known as the Monroe Doctrine (1823) which prohibited any further colonization and intervention by European powers in the Western Hemisphere.

England hoped to replace Spain in establishing her own trading monopoly with these former Spanish colonies. Throughout the 19th century British commercial interests dominated Latin America.

Latin America in Revolution. Inspired by the French Revolution and the Napoleonic period, the rise of Latin American nationalism between 1804 and 1824 would witness the end of three centuries of Spanish colonial rule and the emergence of new heroes such as Toussaint L'Ouverture, Jose San Martin, Bernardo O'Higgins, Simon Bolivar and Miguel Hidalgo.

6.2.2 The Revolutions of the 1820s

Spain (1820 – 1823). Beginning in January, 1820, a mutiny of army troops under Colonel Rafael Riego began in opposition to the persecution of liberals by the restored monarch King Ferdinand VII. The Congress of Verona (1822) authorized a French army to invade Spain and crush the revolutionaries.

Italy (1820 – 1821). Incited to revolution by the activities of secret liberal-nationalist organizations ("carbonari"), liberals revolted in Naples in July 1820 protesting the absolute rule of Ferdinand I of the Kingdom of the Two Sicilies. The Congress of Laibach (1821) authorized Austria to invade and suppress the rebels. An attempted uprising (1821) in Piedmont was crushed by Austrian forces.

The Greek Revolt (1821 – 1830). The revolution which broke out in Greece in 1821, while primarily a nationalist uprising rather than a liberal revolution, was part of a larger problem known as "The Eastern Question." Greece was part of the Ottoman Empire whose vast territories were gradually being recessed throughout the 18th and early 19th centuries. The weakness of the Ottoman Empire and the political and economic ramifications of this instability for the balance of power in Europe kept the major powers in a nervous state of tension.

Because of conflicting interests, the major powers were unable to respond in any harmonious fashion for several years.

The revolt was a leading political question in Europe throughout the 1820s. Occurring in the Romantic era the revolt touched the sensitivities of romantics in the West. A Greek appeal to Christian Europe did not move Prussia or Austria but did fuse England, France and Russia into a united force which defeated a combined Turco-Egyptian naval force at Navarino Bay (1827). Greek independence was recognized through the Treaty of Adrianople (1829).

Russian intervention on the side of Greek revolutionaries was based on Russian national interest (i.e., any dimunition of Ottoman power increased Russian chances of further expansion into the Turkish empire).

Greek nationalism triumphed over the conservative Vienna settlement, and three of the five great powers had aided a movement that violated their agreement of 1815. The self-interests of the great powers demonstrated the growing power of nationalism in the international system.

The Decembrist Uprising in Russia (1825). The death of Alexander I on December 1, 1825 resulted in a crisis over the actual succession to the throne and in turn produced the first significant uprising in Russian history. The expected succession of Constantine, older brother of Alexander I who was believed somewhat more liberal than the late czar, did not materialize. Instead, the younger brother Nicholas, no liberal by any measure, prepared to assume the throne which Constantine had actually renounced.

Hoping to block Nicholas' succession, a group of moderately liberal junior military officers staged a demonstration in late December, 1825 in St. Petersburg only to see it quickly dissipated by artillery attacks ordered by Czar Nicholas I.

The Decembrists were the first upper-class opponents of

the autocratic Russian system of government who called atten-
tion to the popular grievances among Russian society. The insurrection developed in Nicholas I a pathological dislike for
liberal reformers.

A program called "Official Nationality" with the slogan,
"Autocracy, Orthodoxy and National Unity," was designed to
lead Russia back to its historic roots. Through it Nicholas I
became Europe's most reactionary monarch.

Domestically Russia became a police state with censorship
and state-sponsored terrorism. There would be no representative assemblies and education was not only limited but university curricula were carefully monitored. A profound alienation
of Russian intellectual life ensued.

In foreign affairs the same extreme conservatism was demonstrated. The Polish Revolution of 1830 – 31 was crushed and
Russian troops played a key role in stamping out Hungarian
nationalism in the Hapsburg Empire during the revolutionary
uprisings of 1848 – 49. Russia's traditional desire for expansion in the direction of the Ottoman Empire produced a confrontation between France and Russia over who was entitled to
protect Christians and the Holy Places in the Near East. When
the Sultan of Turkey awarded France the honor, Nicholas I was
prepared to go to war against Turkey to uphold Russia's right
to speak for Slavic Christians. The result was the Crimean War
(1854 – 56) which Russia would lose. Nicholas I died (1855)
during the course of fighting this war.

6.2.3 *England Chooses Reform Over Revolution*

The climax of repression in England was the Six Acts of
Parliament (1819). Yet even as these laws were enacted younger
conservative politicians were questioning the wisdom of their
party elders (Wellington, Castlereagh) and calling for modera-

tion. During the 1820s a new group of younger Tories would moderate their party's unbending conservatism.

Liberal Tory Reform, 1822 – 1824. Reform was promoted by George Canning and Robert Peel, in opposition to the reactionary policies of earlier Tory leaders. With the help of liberal Whig politicians enough votes were found to put England on the road to liberal reform.

Canning inaugurated a liberal policy in foreign affairs, including abandonment of the Congress System. Robert Peel reformed prisons and the outdated criminal code as well as establishing an efficient metropolitan police force ("Bobbies").

Mercantile and navigation acts were liberalized enabling British colonies to trade with nations other than England.

The 1673 Test Act, which was a religious test for barring non-Anglicans from participating in the government, was repealed. The Catholic Emancipation Act (1829) granted full civil rights to Roman Catholics, and was prompted by the election of the Irish leader Daniel J. O'Connell to the British Parliament in defiance of the Test Act.

The momentum for liberal reform would continue into the 1830s as Britain realized that accommodation with the new merchant and financial classes was in the spirit of English history. The acid test of liberal reform, however, would come to focus on the willingness of Parliament to repeal the Corn Laws and reform itself.

6.3   REVOLUTIONS II, 1830 – 1833

The Conservative grip on Europe was challenged very quickly following the turbulence of the 1820s, when revolution broke out in France in 1830. By then, the forces of liberalism and nationalism had become so strong that they constituted major threats to the security of many governments. In eastern Europe nationalism was the greater danger while in the West, the demands of middle class liberals for various political reforms grew louder.

6.3.1 *France: The July Revolution*

The death of King Louis XVIII in 1824 brought his brother Charles, Count of Artois and leader of the Ultra Royalists, to the throne as Charles X and set the stage for a return to the Old Regime or revolution.

Attempting to roll back the revolutionary gains, Charles X alienated the moderate forces on the right as well as the entire left in France. Continued violations of the Charter enabled French voters to register their displeasure in the elections of 1827 by giving the liberals a substantial gain in the Chamber of Deputies.

In 1829, when Charles X appointed a ministry led by the Prince of Polignac, the personification of reactionism in France, liberals considered this a declaration of war. Elections in 1830 produced a stunning victory for the liberals. Charles X responded by decreeing the Four Ordinances, which would have amounted to a royal Coup d'État if not stopped. The spark of revolt was set off by the radicals of Paris, with the workers and students raising barricades in the streets with the intention of establishing a republic. Charles X abdicated and fled France.

The Liberals in the Chamber of Deputies, under the leadership of Adolphe Thiers, preferred a constitutional monarchy without a Bourbon ruler. With the cooperation of Talleyrand and Lafayette, they agreed on Prince Louis Philippe, head of the Orleans family and cousin to Charles X.

France was now controlled by the bourgeoisie of upper-middle class bankers and businessmen. King Louis Philippe was "the Bourgeoisie King" who would tilt the government towards these interests. While the July Monarchy of Louis Philippe was politically more liberal than the restoration government, socially it proved to be quite conservative.

The news of the successful July Revolution in France served as a spark ("When France sneezes, the rest of Europe catches cold") to revolutionary uprisings throughout Europe.

6.3.2   The Belgian Independence Movement (1830 – 1831)

Since being merged with Holland in 1815 the upper classes of Belgium never reconciled themselves to rule by a country with a different language, religion and economic life. Inspired by the news of the July Revolution in France, a revolt against Dutch rule broke out in Brussels led by students and industrial workers. The Dutch army was defeated and forced to withdraw from Belgium by the threat of a Franco-British fleet. A national Congress wrote a liberal Belgian Constitution. In 1831 Leopold of Saxe-Coburg (1831 – 1865) became king of the Belgians. In 1839 the Great Powers declared the neutrality of Belgium.

6.3.3   Poland (1830 – 1831)

The new czar of Russia, Nicholas I (reign 1825 – 1855) had his first opportunity to demonstrate his extreme conservatism in foreign policy when a military insurrection broke out late in 1830 in Warsaw. This nationalist uprising challenged the historic Russian domination of Poland. The Russian garrison was driven out of Poland; the czar was deposed as king of Poland; and the independence of Poland was proclaimed by a revolutionary government.

Nicholas I ordered the Russian army to invade Poland; it

ruthlessly proceeded to crush the nationalist rebellion. Poland became "a land of graves and crosses." The Organic Statute of 1832 declared Poland to be an integral part of the Russian empire.

6.3.4 *Italy (1831 – 1832)*

Outbreaks of liberal discontent occurred in northern Italy centering on Modena, Parma, and the Papal States. The inspiration for Italian nationalists who spoke of a unification process was (1) Guiseppe Mazzini and his secret revolutionary society called Young Italy; and (2) the Carbonari, the secret nationalist societies which advocated the use of force to achieve national unification. Still too disorganized, the Italian revolutionaries were easily crushed by Austrian troops under Metternich's enforcement of the Concert of Europe's philosophy. Still, the Italian Risorgimento (resurgence of the Italian spirit) was well under way.

6.3.5 *Germany (1830 – 1833)*

The Carlsbad Decrees of 1819 had effectively restricted freedom throughout Germany. At the news of France's July Revolution, German university students and professors led street demonstrations which forced temporary granting of constitutions in several minor states. These expressions of liberal sentiment and nationalistic desires for German unification were easily crushed by Metternich's domination of the German Confederation (Bund) and his influence over Prussia.

6.3.6 *Great Britain: Reform Continues*

The death of King George IV and the accession of King William IX in 1830 resulted in a general parliamentary election in which the opposition political party, the Whigs, scored major gains with their platform calling for parliamentary reform.

With the Tory party divided, the king asked the leader of the Whig party, Earl Grey (1764 – 1845) to form a government.

Immediately, a major reform bill was introduced designed to increase the number of voters by fifty percent and to eliminate underpopulated electoral districts ("Rotten Boroughs") and replace them with representatives for the previously unrepresented manufacturing districts and cities.

After a national debate, new elections, and a threat from King William IV to alter the composition of the House of Lords, the Great Reform Bill of 1832 was enacted into law. While the Reform Bill did not resolve all political inequities in British political life it marked a new beginning. Several more notable reforms would begin to redraw the sociological landscape of British life.

6.4 EVALUATION

Neither the forces of revolution nor those of reaction were able to maintain the upper hand between 1789 and 1848. Liberalism and nationalism, socialism and democracy were on the march but the forces of conservatism and reaction were still strong enough to contain them. The polarization of Europe was becoming ever so clear: the liberal middle class West, which advocated constitutionalism and industrial progress; and the authoritarian East, which was committed to preserving the status quo. The confrontation would continue until one or the other side would win out decisively.

CHAPTER 7

THE REVOLUTIONS OF 1848

The year 1848 is considered the watershed of the 19th century. The revolutionary disturbances of the first half of the 19th century reached a climax in a new wave of revolutions that extended from Scandinavia to southern Italy and from France to Central Europe. Only England, Russia, and Sweden-Norway avoided violent upheaval.

The issues were substantially the same as they had been in 1789. What was new in 1848 was that these demands were far more widespread and irrepressible than ever before. Whole classes and nations demanded to be fully included in society. The French Revolution of 1789 came at the end of a period ("Ancien Regime") while the revolutions of 1848 signaled the beginning of a new age. Aggravated by a rapid growth in population and social disruption caused by industrialism and urbanization, a massive tide of discontent swept across the Western world.

7.1 CAUSES

Generally speaking, the 1848 upheavals shared in common

the strong influences of romanticism, nationalism, and liberal-ism as well as a new factor of economic dislocation and insta-bility throughout most of Europe. Some authorities believe that it was the absence of liberty that was most responsible for the uprisings.

Specifically, a number of similar conditions existed in sev-eral countries:

1) severe food shortages caused by poor harvests of grain and potatoes (e.g., Irish Potato Famine);

2) financial crises caused by a downturn in the commercial and industrial economy;

3) business failures;

4) widespread unemployment;

5) a sense of frustration and discontent of urban artisan and working classes as wages diminished; a system of poor relief which became overburdened; and living con-ditions which deteriorated in the cities;

6) middle class predominance with the unregulated econ-omy continued to drive these liberals to push for more reform of government and civil liberty by enlisting the help of the working classes in order to put more pres-sure on government to change; and

7) the power of nationalism in the Germanies and Italies as well as Eastern Europe to inspire the overthrow of existing governments.

7.2 REPUBLICANISM: VICTORY IN FRANCE AND DEFEAT IN ITALY

7.2.1 France: The Second Republic and Louis Napoleon

Working class discontent and liberals' unhappiness with the corrupt regime of King Louis Philippe (reign 1830 – 1848) – especially his minister Guizot – erupted in street riots in Paris on February 22 – 23, 1848. With the workers in control of Paris, King Louis Philippe abdicated on February 24 and a provisional government proclaimed the Second French Republic.

Heading the provisional government was the liberal Alphonse Lamartine (1790 – 1869) who favored a moderate republic and political democracy. Lamartine's bourgeoisie allies had little sympathy for the working poor and did not intend to pursue a social revolution as well.

The working class groups were united by their leader Louis Blanc (1811 – 1882), a socialist thinker who expected the provisional government to deal with the unemployed and anticipated the power of the state being used to improve life and the conditions of labor. Pressed by the demands of Blanc and his followers, the provisional government established national workshops to provide work and relief for thousands of unemployed workers.

The "June Days" revolution was provoked when the government closed the national workshop. A general election in April resulted in a National Assembly dominated by the moderate republicans and conservatives under Lamartine who regarded socialist ideas as threats to private property. The Parisian workers, feeling that their revolution had been nullified, took to the streets in revolution.

This new revolution (June 23 – 26) was unlike previous

uprisings in France. It marked the inauguration of genuine class warfare; it was a revolt against poverty and a cry for the redistribution of property. It foreshadowed the great social revolutions of the 20th century. The revolt was extinguished after General Cavaignac was given dictatorial powers by the government. The June Days confirmed the political predominance of conservative property holders in French life.

The new Constitution of the Second French Republic provided for a unicameral legislative (with the National Assembly designating themselves as the first members) and executive power vested in a popularly-elected president of the Republic. When the election returns were counted the candidate of the government, General Cavaignac, was soundly defeated by a "dark horse" candidate, Prince Louis Napoleon Bonaparte (1808 – 1873), a nephew of the great emperor. On December 20, 1848, Louis Napoleon was installed as President of the republic.

It was clear the voters turned to the name of Bonaparte as a source of stability and greatness. They expected him to prevent any further working class disorder. However, the election of Louis Napoleon doomed the Second Republic. He was a Bonaparte, and dedicated to his own fame and vanity and not republican institutions. In December 1852 Louis Napoleon became Emperor Napoleon III and France retreated from republicanism again.

7.2.2 Italy: Republicanism Defeated

Italian nationalists and liberals wanted to end Hapsburg (Austrian), Bourbon (Naples and Sicily), and papal domination and unite these disparate areas into a unified liberal nation. A revolt by liberals in Sicily in January, 1848 was followed by the granting of liberal constitutions in Naples, Tuscany, Piedmont, and the Papal States. Milan and Venice expelled their

Austrian rulers. In March, 1848, upon hearing the news of the revolution in Vienna, a fresh outburst of revolution from Austrian rule occurred in Lombardy and Venetia with Sardinia-Piedmont declaring war on Austria. Simultaneously, Italian patriots attacked the Papal States forcing the Pope, Pius IX, to flee to Naples for refuge.

The temporary nature of these initial successes was illustrated by the speed with which the conservative forces regained control. In the north, Austrian Field Marshal Radetsky swept aside all opposition, regaining Lombardy and Venetia and crushing Sardinia-Piedmont. In the Papal States, the establishment of the Roman Republic (February 1849) under the leadership of Giuseppe Mazzini and the protection of Giuseppe Garibaldi, would fail when French troops took Rome in July 1849 after a heroic defense by Garibaldi. Pope Pius IX returned to Rome cured of his liberal leanings. In the south and in Sicily the revolts were suppressed by the former rulers.

Within eighteen months the revolutions of 1848 had failed throughout Italy. Among the explanations for these failures were the failure of conservative rural people to support the revolution; the divisions in aim and technique among the revolutionaries; the fear the radicals aroused among moderate groups of Italians who would be needed to guarantee the success of any revolution; and the general lack of experience and administrative ability on the part of the revolutionists.

7.3 NATIONALISM RESISTED IN AUSTRIAN EMPIRE

The Hapsburg Empire was vulnerable to revolutionary challenge. With its collection of subject nationalities (more non-Germans than Germans), the empire was stirred by an acute spirit of nationalism; its government was reactionary (liberal institutions were non-existent); and its social reliance on serf-dom doomed the masses of people to a life without hope. As soon as news of the "February Days" in France reached the borders of the Austrian Empire, rebellions began. The long-suppressed opponents of the government believed the time had come to introduce liberal institutions into the empire.

7.3.1 *Vienna*

In March, 1848, Hungarian criticism of Hapsburg imperial rule was initiated by Magyar nationalist leader Louis Kossuth (1802 – 1894), who demanded Hungarian independence. Students and workers in Vienna rushed to the streets to demonstrate on behalf of a more liberal government. The army failed to restore order and Prince Metternich, the symbol of reaction, resigned and fled the country. Emperor Ferdinand I (reign 1835 – 1848) granted a moderately liberal constitution but its shortcomings dissatisfied more radical elements and continual disorder prompted the emperor to flee from Vienna to Innsbruck, where he relied on his army commanders to restore order in the Empire. The Austrian imperial troops remained loyal to the Hapsburg crown. Prince Schwarzenberg was put in charge of restoring Hapsburg control.

A people's committee ruled Vienna where a liberal assembly gathered to write a constitution. In Hungary and Bohemia revolutionary outbreaks indicated ultimate success.

The inability of the revolutionary groups in Vienna to govern effectively made it easier for the Hapsburgs to lay siege to Vienna in October, 1848. The rebels surrendered and Emperor Ferdinand abdicated in favor of his eighteen-year-old nephew, Francis Joseph (reign 1848 – 1916), who promptly restored royal absolutism.

The imperial government had been saved at Vienna through

the loyalty of the army and the lack of ruling capacity on the part of the revolutionaries. The only thing the revolutionaries could agree on was their hatred of the Hapsburg dynasty.

7.3.2 Bohemia

Nationalist feeling among the Czechs or Bohemians had been smoldering for centuries. They demanded a constitution and autonomy within the Hapsburg Empire.

A Pan-Slav Congress attempted to unite all Slavic peoples but accomplished little because divisions were more decisive among them than unified opposition to Hapsburg control.

In June, 1848, Prague submitted to a military occupation followed by a military dictatorship in July after all revolutionary groups were crushed.

7.3.3 Hungary

The Kingdom of Hungary was a state of about twelve million under Hapsburg authority. Magyars or Hungarians, who represented about five million subjects of the emperor, enjoyed a privileged position in the empire. The remaining seven million Slavic and Rumanian natives were powerless.

In March, 1848 Nationalist leader Louis Kossuth took over direction of the movement and tamed a more radical Hungarian rebellion; Hungarian autonomy was declared in April but failed to win popular support for the revolution because of the tyrannical treatment of the Slavic minorities. Because the government in Vienna was distracted by revolutions everywhere in the empire in the summer and fall of 1848, Louis Kossuth had time to organize an army to fight for Hungarian independence.

War between Austria and Hungary was declared on October 3, 1848 and Hungarian armies drove to within sight of Vienna. But desperate resistance from Slavic minorities forced the Hungarians to withdraw. Hungary was invaded by an Austrian army from the West in June, 1849 and a Russian army (Tsar Nicholas I of Russia offered assistance to new emperor Francis Joseph) from the north. Along with Serbian resistance in the south and Rumanian resistance in the east the combined opposition proved too much for Louis Kossuth's Hungarian Republic (proclaimed in April 1849) which was defeated. Kossuth fled into exile while thirteen of his guards were executed. Not until Austria was defeated by Prussia in 1866 would Hungary be in a position again to demand governmental equality with the Austrians.

7.3.4 *Italy*

Charles Albert, King of Sardinia, having granted his people a constitution, and hoping to add the Hapsburgs' Italian holdings to his kingdom, declared war on Austria. Unfortunately, the Sardinian army was twice defeated in battle (Custozza and Novara) by the Austrian General Radetsky.

King Charles Albert abdicated in favor of his son, Victor Emmanuel, who was destined to complete the unification of Italy in the second half of the 19th century.

The Revolutions of 1848 failed in Austria for these reasons:

1) The subject nationalities sometimes hated each other more than they despised Austria. The Hapsburgs used the divisions between the ethnic groups as an effective weapon against each: Croats against Magyars and Serbs and Rumanians against Magyars in the Hungarian Revolution; Germans against Czechs in the revolt in Bohemia.

2) The imperial army had remained loyal to its aristocratic commanders who favored absolutism.

3) There were too few industrial workers and an equally small number of middle class. The industrial workers could not exert any political power and the middle class feared working-class radicalism and rallied to the government as defender of the status quo.

7.4 LIBERALISM HALTED IN THE GERMANIES

The immediate effect of the 1848 Revolution in France was a series of liberal and nationalistic demonstrations in the German states (March, 1848) with the rulers promising liberal concessions. The liberals' demand for constitutional government was coupled with another demand: some kind of union or federation of the German states. While popular demonstrations by students, workers, and the middle class produced the promise of a liberal future the permanent success or failure of these "promises" rested on Prussian reaction.

7.4.1 *Prussia, The Frankfurt Parliament and German Unification*

Under King Frederick William IV (reign 1848 – 1861) Prussia moved from revolution to reaction. After agreeing to liberalize the Prussian government following street rioting in Berlin, the king rejected the constitution written by a specially-called assembly. The liberal ministry resigned and was replaced by a conservative one. By the fall the king felt powerful enough to substitute his own constitution, which guaranteed royal control of the government with a complicated three-class system of indirect voting that excluded all but landlords and wealthy bourgeoisie from office. This system prevailed in Prussia until 1918.

Finally, the government ministry was responsible to the king and the military services swore loyalty to the king alone.

Self appointed liberal, romantic, and nationalist leaders called for elections to a constituent assembly from all states belonging to the German Bund for the purpose of unifying the German states. Meeting in May, 1848, the Frankfurt Parliament was composed of mostly intellectuals, professionals, lawyers, businessmen and middle class. After a year of deliberation over questions of (1) monarchy or republic; (2) federal union or centralized state; and (3) boundaries (i.e., only German-populated or mixed nationalities), the assembly produced a constitution.

The principal problem facing the Frankfurt Assembly was to obtain Prussian support. The smaller German states generally favored the Frankfurt Constitution as did liberals throughout the large and middle-sized states. Austria made it clear it was opposed to the work of the Assembly and would remain in favor of the present system.

The Assembly leaders made the decision to stake their demands for a united Germany on King Frederick William IV of Prussia. They selected him as emperor in April 1849 only to have him reject the offer because he was a divine-right monarch, not subject to popularly-elected assemblies. Without Prussia there could be no success, so the Frankfurt Parliament dissolved without achieving a single accomplishment.

The Prussian King Frederick William IV had his own plans for uniting Germany. Right after refusing a "crown from the gutter" he offered his own plan to the German princes wherein Prussia would play a prominent role along with Austria. When Austria demanded allegiance to the Bund, the Prussian king realized pushing his plan would involve him in a war with Austria and her allies (including Russia). In November, 1850,

Prussia agreed to forego the idea of uniting the German states at a meeting with Austria called the "Humiliation of Olmutz." Austrian domination of the German Bund was confirmed.

7.5   GREAT BRITAIN AND THE VICTORIAN COMPROMISE

The Victorian Age (1837 – 1901) is associated with the long reign of Queen Victoria, who succeeded her uncle, King William IV at the age of eighteen and married her cousin, Prince Albert. The early years of her reign coincided with the continuation of liberal reform of the British government accomplished through an arrangement known as the "Victorian Compromise." The Compromise was a political alliance of the middle class and aristocracy to exclude the working class from political power. The middle class gained control of the House of Commons, the aristocracy controlled the government, army, and Church of England. The process of accommodation was working successfully.

7.5.1   *Highlights of the "Compromise Era"*

Parliamentary reforms continued after passage of the 1832 Reform Bill. Laws were enacted abolishing slavery throughout the Empire (1833). The Factory Act (1831) forbade the employment of children under age of nine. The New Poor Law (1834) now required the needy who were able and unemployed to live in workhouses. The Municipal Reform Law (1835) gave control of the cities to the middle class. The last remnants of the mercantilistic age fell with the abolition of the Corn Laws (1846) and repeal of the old navigation acts (1849).

Working class protest arose in the wake of their belief that passage of the "Great Reform Bill" of 1832 would bring them prosperity. When workers found themselves no better off, they turned to collective action of a political nature. They linked the solution of their economic plight to a program of political reform known as Chartism or the Chartist movement from the charter of six points which they petitioned Parliament to adopt:

1) universal male suffrage,

2) secret ballot for voting,

3) no property qualifications for members of Parliament,

4) salaries for members of Parliament,

5) annual elections for Parliament, and

6) equal electoral districts.

During the age of Victorian Compromise these ideas were considered dangerously radical. Both the middle class and aristocracy vigorously opposed the working class political agenda. Chartism as a national movement failed. Its ranks were split between those who favored violence and those who advocated peaceful tactics. The return of prosperity with steady wages and lower food prices robbed the movement of momentum. Yet the chartist movement came to constitute the first large-scale working class political movement that workers everywhere would eventually adopt if they were to improve their situation.

After 1846 England was more and more dominated by the middle class; this was one of the factors which enabled England to escape the revolutions which shook Europe in 1848. The ability of the English to make meaningful industrial reforms gave the working class hope that its goals could be achieved without violent social upheaval.

7.6 EVALUATION

The revolutions of 1848 began with much promise, but they all ended in defeat for a number of reasons:

1) They were spontaneous movements which lost their popular support as the people lost their enthusiasm. Initial successes by the revolutionaries were due less to their strength than to the hesitancy of governments to use their superior force. Once this hesitancy was overcome, the revolutions were smashed.

2) They were essentially urban movements, and the conservative landowners and peasants tended in time to nullify the spontaneous actions of the urban classes.

3) The middle class, who led the revolutions, came to fear the radicalism of their working class allies. While in favor of political reformation, the middle class drew the line at social engineering much to the dismay of the laboring poor.

4) Divisions among national groups, and the willingness of one nationality to deny rights to other nationalities, helped to destroy the revolutionary movements in central Europe.

However, the results of 1848 – 1849 were not entirely negative. Universal male suffrage was introduced in France; serfdom remained abolished in Austria and the German states; parliaments were established in Prussia and other German states, dominated, to be sure, by princes and aristocrats; and Prussia and Sardinia-Piedmont emerged with new determination to succeed in their respective unification schemes.

The Revolutions of 1848 – 1849 brought to a close the era

of liberal revolutions that had begun in France in 1789. Reformers and revolutionists alike learned a lesson from the failures of 1848. They learned that planning and organization is necessary; that rational argument and revolution would not always assure success. With 1848 the Age of Revolution sputtered out. The Age of Romanticism was about to give way to an Age of Realism.

CHAPTER 8

EPILOGUE: THE VIEW FROM MID-NINETEENTH CENTURY EUROPE

A new age was about to follow the Revolutions of 1848-1849 as Otto von Bismarck, one of the dominant political figures of the second half of the 19th century, was quick to realize. If the mistake of these years was to believe that great decisions could be brought about by speeches and parliamentary majorities, the sequel would soon show that in an industrial era new techniques involving ruthless force were all too readily available. The period of Realpolitik — of realistic, iron-fisted politics and diplomacy — was about to happen.

By 1850 all humankind was positioned to become part of a single worldwide interacting whole. Based on military technology and industrial productivity, no part of the world could prevent Europeans from imposing their will.

The half century after 1850 would witness the political consolidation and economic expansion that paved the way for the brief global domination of Europe. The conservative monarchies of Sardinia-Piedmont and Prussia united Italy and Germany by military force and gave birth to new power relationships on the continent. Externalizing their rivalries produced conflict overseas in a new age of imperialism, which saw Africa and Asia fall under the domination of the West.

Nationalism overtook liberalism as the dominant force in human affairs after 1850. Nationalists would be less romantic and more hardheaded. The good of the nation and not the individual became the new creed. The state would be deified.

After 1848 – 1849 the middle class ceased to be revolutionary. It became concerned about protecting its hard-earned political power and property rights against radical political and social movements. And the working classes also adopted new tactics and organizations. They turned to trade unions and political parties to achieve their political and social goals.

A great era of human progress was about to begin — material, political, scientific, industrial, social and cultural — shaping of the contours of the world.

"The ESSENTIALS" of HISTORY

REA's **Essentials of History** series offers a new approach to the study of history that is different from what has been available previously. Compared with conventional history outlines, the **Essentials of History** offer far more detail, with fuller explanations and interpretations of historical events and developments. Compared with voluminous historical tomes and textbooks, the **Essentials of History** offer a far more concise, less ponderous overview of each of the periods they cover.

The **Essentials of History** provide quick access to needed information, and will serve as handy reference sources at all times. The **Essentials of History** are prepared with REA's customary concern for high professional quality and student needs.

UNITED STATES HISTORY
1500 to 1789 From Colony to Republic
1789 to 1841 The Developing Nation
1841 to 1877 Westward Expansion & the Civil War
1877 to 1912 Industrialism, Foreign Expansion & the Progressive Era
1912 to 1941 World War I, the Depression & the New Deal
America since 1941: Emergence as a World Power

EUROPEAN HISTORY
1450 to 1648 The Renaissance, Reformation & Wars of Religion
1648 to 1789 Bourbon, Baroque & the Enlightenment
1789 to 1848 Revolution & the New European Order
1848 to 1914 Realism & Materialism
1914 to 1935 World War I & Europe in Crisis
Europe since 1935: From World War II to the Demise of Communism

WORLD HISTORY
Ancient History (4500 BC to AD 500)
The Emergence of Western Civilization
Medieval History (AD 500 to 1450)
The Middle Ages

CANADIAN HISTORY
Pre-Colonization to 1867
The Beginning of a Nation
1867 to Present
The Post-Confederate Nation

If you would like more information about any of these books,
complete the coupon below and return it to us or visit your local bookstore.

RESEARCH & EDUCATION ASSOCIATION
61 Ethel Road W. • Piscataway, New Jersey 08854
Phone: (732) 819-8880

Please send me more information about your History Essentials books

Name _____

Address _____

City _____ State _____ Zip _____